TOPICS

In Jazz Bass

Volume 1
HARMONY

Danny Ziemann

©2018 Danny Ziemann

©2018 Danny Ziemann
All Rights Reserved.

No part of this publication may be reproduced,
stored in retrieval system, or transmitted, in any form or by any means,
electronic, mechanical, photocopying, recording or otherwise,
without prior written permission from Danny Ziemann.

ISBN-13: 978-0-692-17205-6

Editing: Erik Piazza
Cover Design: Alison Cote
Interior Layout: Matthew Burg
Music Engraver: Marc Schwartz
Biography Photo: Tomas Flint
Back Cover Photo: Laura Pleifer
Consultant: John Fetter
Audio Engineer: Matt Ramerman at Green Room Studios, Rochester NY
Guitar: Chris Potter
Drums: Chase Ellison

To access supplemental audio, please visit **www.dannyziemann.com.**

Acknowledgements

In loving memory of my father Kenneth, a man who dedicated his life to his family. The realization of my dreams would not have been possible without your love and support.

Special thanks to…

Erik Piazza—thank you for your sharp eyes, ears, and strong editorial expertise. Working on this with you was a joy, and you truly brought these concepts to life!

John Fetter—thank you for your mentorship and consulting with me in the early stages of writing.

Conny Habacher—your encouragement has been a treasure to me throughout the completion of this project. Thank you for continually pushing me to be my best.

This publication was funded in part by grants from the Institute for Music Leadership at the Eastman School of Music and the Eastman Community Music School. Thank you to both institutions for your generous support.

About the Author

Danny Ziemann is a bassist and educator living in Rochester, NY. A graduate of the Eastman School of Music, Danny has been freelancing regularly since the age of 16. He has toured extensively throughout North America, Europe, and Asia with bandleader Gordon Webster. Danny was the bassist in the first Focusyear Artist Diploma band, in Basel, Switzerland, where he spent one year studying and playing with luminaries including Larry Grenadier, Dave Holland, Joshua Redman, Kurt Rosenwinkel, Jorge Rossy, and others. During breaks in his touring schedule, Danny records session bass, and serves as a first-call bassist in Western New York. In both 2015 and 2017, he placed 2nd in the International Society of Bassists jazz bass competition.

In addition to a full performing schedule, Danny is a dedicated educator. His two jazz bass method books, The Low Down Vol. 1 & 2, have received continuous acclaim in the bass community. Danny is an active clinician, working with students at universities and high schools and presenting at various conferences held both in the US and abroad. He also produced two courses on jazz bass performance as a tutor for the website Discover Double Bass. Danny currently teaches at The Eastman Community Music School, SUNY Oswego, and is a visiting professor of jazz bass at the Eastman School of Music.

Table of Contents

Note from the Editor 1
Preface 3

Chapter 1 — Exploring the Relationship Between Tonic and Dominant in Static Harmony 5
Introduction 6
Exercises 10, 31
Samples 21
Full Walking Samples 35

Chapter 2 — Adapting I-V-I to Harmony of Two Bars Length 53
Introduction 54
Exercises 57, 65
Samples 67
Full Walking Samples 72

Chapter 3 — Triadic ii-V-I Shapes 81
Introduction 82
Exercises 90, 103, 112
Samples 113
Fulll Walking Samples 120

Chapter 4 — Reduction Harmony 131
Introduction 132
Exercises 141, 153
Full Walking Samples 160

Chapter 5 — Reduction Harmony II: Rhythm Changes 171
Introduction 172
Exercises 183
Full Walking Samples 187

Note from the Editor

You do not have to be a bass player to understand and apply the harmonic ideas presented in these chapters, yet even the most skilled bass players will find these concepts relevant and valuable. Danny's approach to functional jazz bass harmony is simple and well-defined, and the carefully constructed exercises provide endless practice material. This book is immediately applicable and bound to have a lasting impact on how you and your students approach jazz bass harmony.

I am honored to have been asked to work on this book, and I hope my contributions have helped to make Danny's ideas and concepts more clear and accessible.

–Erik Piazza

Preface

Since publishing the Low Down Vol. 1 & 2, my interest in studying and teaching the art of walking bass has grown with fervor. I believe thorough examination of walking bass can teach one more about fingerboard geography and harmonic function than many areas of musical study. Learning walking bass includes transcribing, improvising, composing, learning melodies, and developing a beautiful sound; all skills that contribute to building the whole musician. It also instills a sense of musical empathy, reinforcing "How can I say the most while playing the least?" Through study of walking bass, students soon begin to demonstrate two necessary components to being a musician: awareness of how harmony functions through the instrument, and how they relate to other musicians in a group setting.

One question I've often asked of my own musicianship is: "How can I create the most informed bass lines with the most basic harmonic information?" What does informed mean exactly? Simply put, being able to play with total harmonic awareness and understanding the implications of every note choice to avoid interfering with the melody, comping instruments, or soloist. I'd like to imply in one note what a pianist does in five—with the same intent and understanding. It's easier to influence the shape and direction of music when you have control over the most fundamental choices first. Topics in Jazz Bass: Harmony is born out of the desire to develop total harmonic control.

The idea of harmonic simplification came together after years of reflecting on my performance experiences and lessons with mentors, learning piano, and composing bass lines. Though I am not currently aware of pedagogy in the bass world addressing similar ideas, Barry Harris and his teachings were an influence on much of my conception of harmony. Please watch his videos online if you have not already—they are timeless.

This book assumes the reader is familiar with the the bass and has fundamental walking skills. Be sure to spend plenty of time exploring each concept. Though initial core concepts will be reinforced in each chapter, they need time to sink in and form a big picture. As a part of your practice, it is imperative that you compose bass lines to better understand these concepts, and learn the melody to as many tunes as you can —these tasks will solidify your walking vocabulary and guide your note choices.

No one book or source has the answer. Books are a tool. There are many great tools available to guide your learning; treat them all as a supplements to one another. And while these concepts will deepen your understanding of walking bass, there is simply no substitute for listening and transcribing jazz greats. Many questions can be answered by spending time absorbing the lineage of recorded jazz history. As you practice and play, find ways to infuse the concepts from this book into the more traditional bass vocabulary. For any instrumentalist, a wide palette of harmonic color and vocabulary will have the greatest impact.

Please know that it is a privilege to join you on your musical journey—thank you for trusting me to lead you further.

Chapter 1

Exploring the Relationship Between
Tonic and Dominant in Static Harmony

Chapter 1

Many bassists are on a mission to create hip sounding bass lines. They aim to avoid cliché and repetitive patterns by adding chromaticism and rhythmic interest while obscuring the more obvious pillar points in the song. These variables can add sophistication, but may also have the detrimental effect of obscuring voice leading and pulse. Without forethought, the result is an unclear and unsupportive bass line which, to the trained ear, lacks of musical direction. In the right context, these types of colorful additions can certainly enhance the quality of a bass line; in the wrong context, chromaticism and rhythmic additions become disruptive and distracting.

The desire to elevate the hip factor should be viewed through a different lens: clear execution of the most fundamental harmonies—in an appropriate range—that provides the ability to influence overall density of sound and shape of the music. Instead of looking outside of the chord, what if bassists explored the most basic diatonic information and their implications as a means of sounding hip?

The fundamental responsibility of the bass player is to provide a supportive foundation. Only when you understand this can you deviate from that role (while understanding what you're deviating from, and why). This type of acute awareness contributes greater support than extra chromaticism or rhythmic additions. When you fully understand how each note you play relates to the present chord, the notes before and after it in a linear sense, and the implied notes directly above and below it (i.e. does the C# you played over a BbMaj7 chord imply C# Diminished?), you'll gain a sense for how bass lines influence and interact with the whole musical picture.

One way to develop this awareness is to dig into the relationship between tonic and dominant functions. To start, we will apply a label of tonic or dominant to each note in the major or minor scale. Then we will apply the concept to static major or minor tonic chords (the same chord occurring for three or more bars without change). You will learn to use three-note triadic shapes to represent alternating tonic and dominant harmonies.

I will briefly discuss how to manipulate this concept to two-bar static harmony, but you will learn how to manipulate these techniques to fit harmonies of different lengths in later chapters. These shapes will help you better visualize harmonic movement and show the implied harmonic function of your note choices.

A Common Walking Pitfall:

A familiar blues bass line might look like this, though you may not have considered the implied harmonic movement listed underneath. This is one possible harmonization using basic techniques:

Example 1a

Excessive chromaticism throughout the entire bass line can be a common walking pitfall. Though seemingly insignificant, every note has an effect on the harmony—and the pianist, guitarist, and soloist who interact with it. While a bassist might not think anything of a "B" passing tone to Bb7 in measure four of the blues, the pianist who voices a beautiful Fm11 now sounds wrong and has to adjust accordingly.

The same linear and chromatic approach might be taken with tunes like "Smile" and "All The Things You Are," with similar implications. Examples 1b and 1c are not bad bass lines—nor should you avoid this material—they merely should be played with proper understanding of the implied harmony.

Example 1b - "Smile"

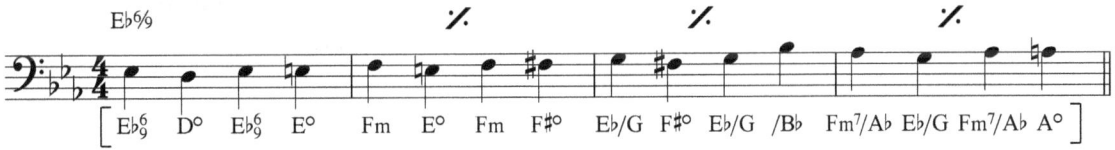

Example 1c - "All The Things You Are"

There are examples where I use chromaticism to move to the next chord change—particularly the root—and this can be unavoidable at moments. Chromaticism plays a strong role in the creation of walking vocabulary, but one must be aware of how it functions in context to make the most impact on the line.

This level of awareness is where pianists and guitarists live all the time. In essence, we are applying the most basic principles of comping to walking bass lines. When a pianist comps, they commonly think of the top note as melody and apply a basic harmonization underneath. The melody line in Example 1d follows scale degrees (now referred to as SD) "1-2-3-4-5" in both major and minor tonalities. The most simple and effective way to harmonize is by alternating between tonic and dominant functions:

Example 1d

The diminished chord implies dominant functionality; another way of viewing it is G7b9. This type of harmonization technique effectively assigns a value of either dominant (V) or tonic (I) to any note in a major or minor scale. This allows any note to be harmonized while comping.

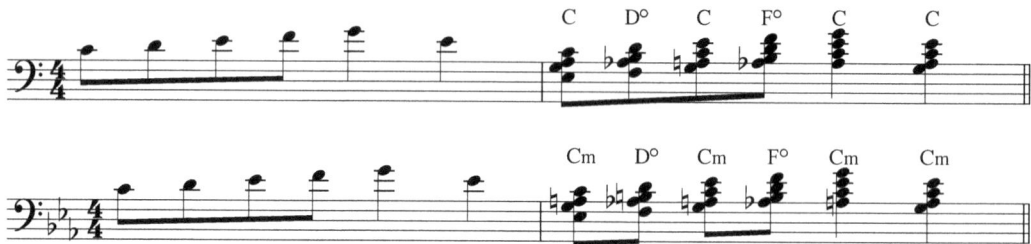

The following exercises will apply similar principles to help you better understand how different note choices function in a walking bass line. Every note—chromatic and diatonic—has an implied harmony. With practice, you can apply the same level of clarity and understanding as comping instrumentalists to your bass lines. The exercises in this chapter will teach you to improvise three moving counterpoint lines at the same time—lines that you can both see visually and understand aurally.

The exercises and chord shapes in this chapter follow a consistent set of guidelines:
They fit in the hand well and require minimal shifting. You can typically play them in a span of a half step.
They allow for easy travel through the bass, covering a left hand spacing of three strings. This facilitates simultaneous linear and vertical movement with ease of visualization.

These exercises will provide harmonic clarity and extremely melodic bass lines with unique vocabulary.

Conceptualizing I-V-I movement:

Major scales are commonly associated with the following harmonies:

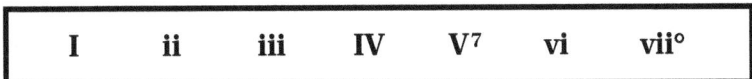

Example 2a

Example 2a shows this harmonization applied to the G Major scale.

This harmonization, while theoretically correct, contains many functions—far too many to think about while walking bass lines.

Example 2b

This demonstrates how the major scale can be reharmonized by alternating the notes of the tonic triad (I) and dominant 7 chord (V7) [with the subdominant chord (IV) on scale degree 6].

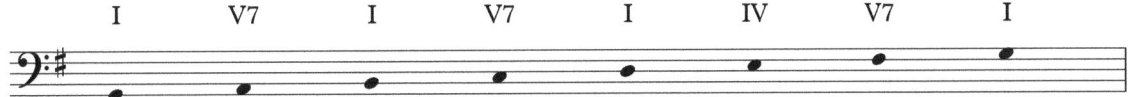

The dominant function is only applied to notes in between those containing tonic functionality [scale degrees 2, 4, and 7].

Example 2c

This basic harmonization is much easier to keep in mind than the harmonization in Example 2a—each note contains one of two functions [three, including subdominant].

Exercises

The major scale will be limited to the first five notes, focusing on the first two patterns of the tonic-dominant-tonic relationship. From now on, this will be referred to as the I-V-I device.

Exercise 1

This exercise is based on scale degrees (SD) 1-2-3 of the tonic. In Pattern 1, SD 1-2-3 occurs in the bass (lowest) voice. In Pattern 2, SD 1-2-3 occurs in the melody (highest) voice. The key and register of the bass will determine whether it is most appropriate to conceptualize the harmonic movement in the melody or bass voice.

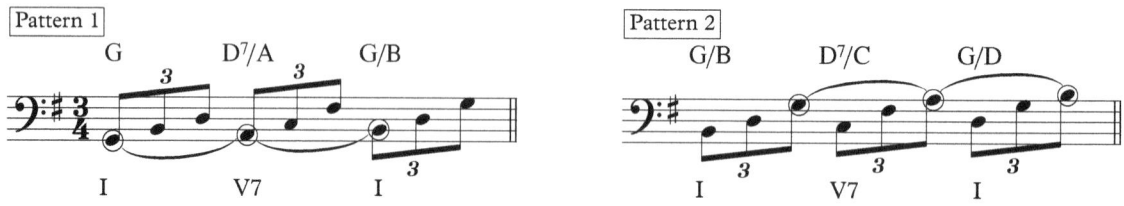

In the first pattern, SD 1-2-3 are emphasized in the bass motion. In the second pattern, they are emphasized in the melody motion.

Exercise 2

Patterns 1 and 2 are the same as in Exercise 1, but in minor tonality. Dominant patterns in major and minor tonalities function exactly the same.

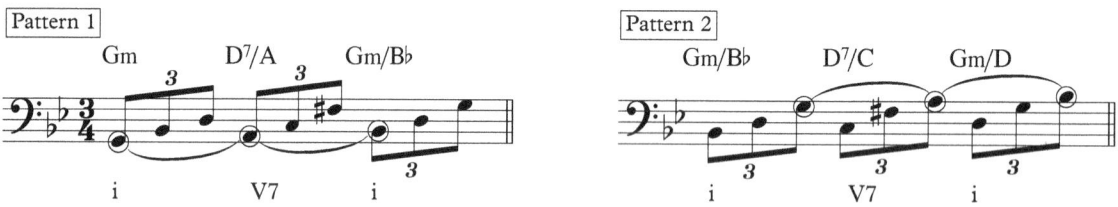

Exercise 3a - Ascending Major

The following exercise ascends through patterns 1 and 2 in major tonalities. Start by practicing these at quarter note = 60 bpm on the metronome. Take note of which positions have similar fingerings. Once you are familiar with one set of fingerings, look for alternate paths through the exercises. Practice these in thumb position if you are able.

Exercise 3b - Ascending Minor

The following exercise ascends through patterns 1 and 2 in minor tonalities. Start by practicing these at quarter note = 60 bpm on the metronome. Take note of which positions have similar fingerings. Once you are familiar with one set of fingerings, look for alternate paths through the exercises.

Exercise 4a

Though you can ascend and descend through these patterns, ascending patterns in major and minor allows for the smoothest voice leading. Descending Pattern 1—using SD 3-2-1 (or b3-2-1) in the bass voice—leaves the leading tone F# (scale degree 7) unresolved. Deviating away from the pattern is the only way to fulfill the voice leading.

Exercise 4b

Descending Pattern 2—using SD 3-2-1 (or b3-2-1) in the melody voice—presents no voice leading concerns.

Exercise 5a

This exercise combines both I-V-I in major and minor keys. It is conceptualized as SD 1-2-3 (or 1-2-b3) in the melody voice. The V7 chord starts on SD 2 of the tonic key, and pivots between both major and minor tonalities. Exercise 5b demonstrates the concept in 12 keys.

Begin with a metronome marking of quarter note equals 50 beats per measure, then increase the tempo as you gain more command. Resolve on the first note of the first measure, and briefly pause before transitioning keys to prepare your ear for the change in tonic.

Exercise 5b - 12 keys

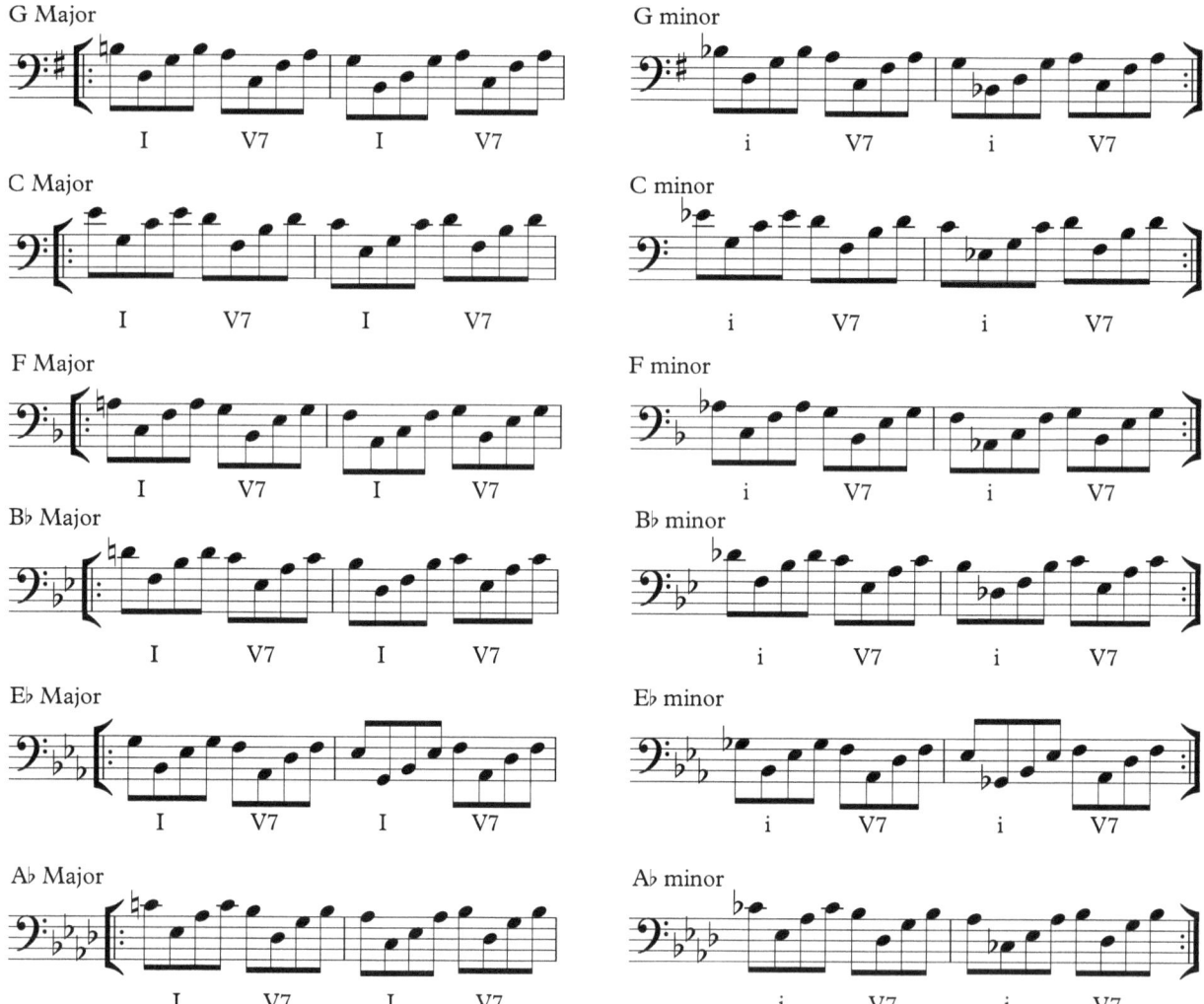

Exercise 6

This variation emphasizes the bass voice, and the treatment of the leading tone is not as smooth. It does not invalidate this line, it just limits the context in which you should use it. The proper resolution is labeled to illustrate the tendency of the leading tone. For your own practice, transpose this exercise into 12 keys with the proper resolution.

Using I-V-I in bass lines:

With this general foundation, you can start incorporating I-V-I movement in your bass lines. The goal is to incorporate more functional harmony over static chords of three bars length or more. Many tunes contain static harmony, including "So What," "Smile," "Bye Bye Blackbird," and "I'll Remember April."
I mentioned earlier that each note in a walking line has a harmonic implication. In the following examples, each note in a measure of tonic function implies tonic functionality, and each note in a measure of dominant function implies dominant functionality.

Example 3a

This example of "Bye Bye Blackbird" contains static harmony: five bars of F Major 7. Though there are many ways to play the first eight bars of this tune, these are the simplest and most closely related to the original changes. This uses SD 1-2-3-2-1 motion in the melody.

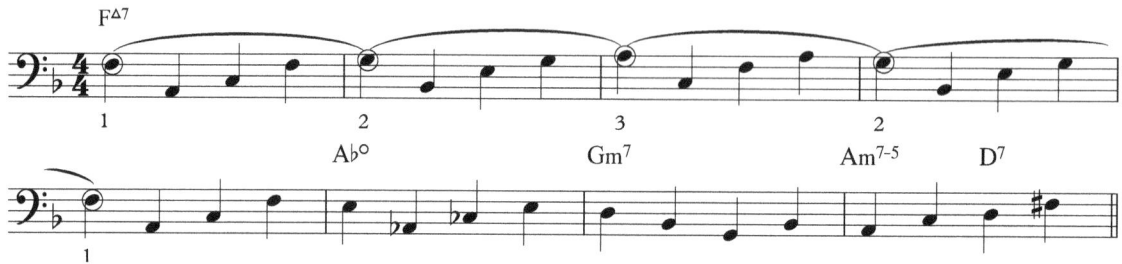

Example 3b

Here is an 8-bar example of a bass line over the tune "Smile." The I-V-I device is used over the Eb6/9 chord in measures 1-5, and uses a 1-2-3-2-1 motion in the melody voice.

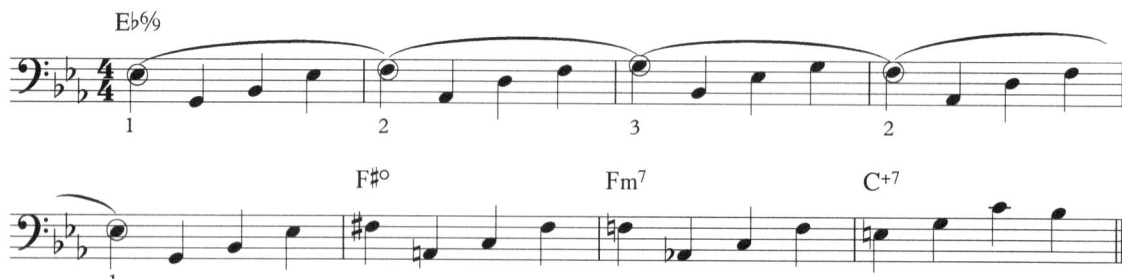

Example 3c

"The Lamp Is Low" uses the I-V-I device over the A Minor 7 chord in measures 1-3, and uses 1-2-1 in the melody motion.

Example 3d

"Just Friends" pivots between major and minor, similar to Exercise 5a. Though the I-V-I device typically only works on static harmony of three or more bars in length, this is a special circumstance as the target resolution—C—still remains the same.

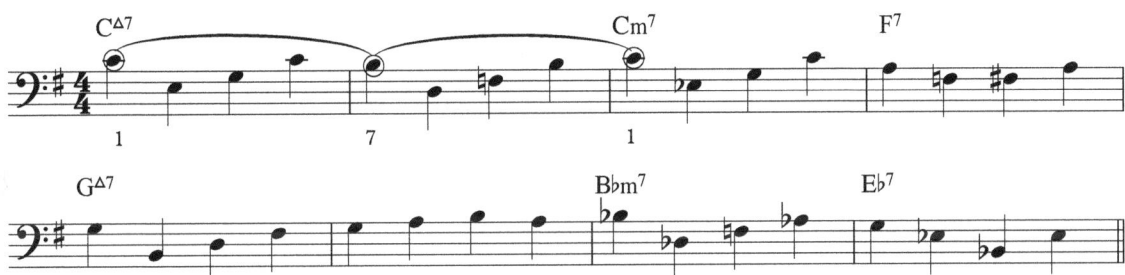

Example 3e

"I'll Remember April" offers an effective way to practice pivoting between major and minor, similar to Exercise 5a.

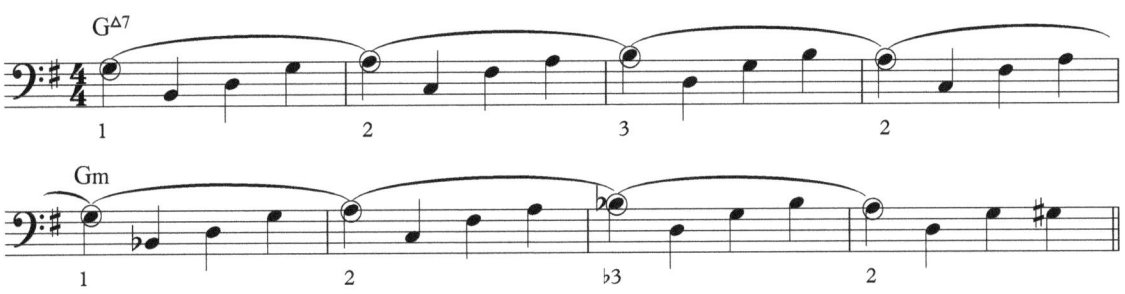

Melodic awareness:

Your usage of this device will change depending on whether you're supporting the melody or a solo. When playing a bass line behind the statement of the melody, a lack of melodic awareness can be a detriment to the overall quality and effectiveness of your line. Even if it is correct and sounds great in isolation from the band, a line that does not consider the melody runs the risk of collapsing the counterpoint.

When using these I-V-I bass lines, the strong beats (1 & 3) can double the melody or create a dissonance—particularly on a tune like "Bye Bye Blackbird." A more supportive bass line would find notes to complement the melody; roots to provide grounding and 3rds/6ths to harmonize where appropriate. Learning the melody is imperative to creating supportive bass lines.

Due to copyright concerns we cannot include melodies to these standards. I would suggest notating the melodies on staff paper and writing bass lines underneath to see the potential clashes.

Sample Bass Lines

I've included sample bass lines that use these principles when possible. Transcribing great bassists, listening to recordings, learning melodies, and writing bass lines are all important pieces of the learning puzzle. These samples highlight the I-V-I device over static harmony, mixed with more conventional vocabulary (scalar based movement, chromaticism to roots, and linear target notes). Minimal analysis is included other than where the instances of I-V-I are used. Assume that these bass lines occur behind solo lines, not the melody.

Sample 1 - "Smile"
Sample 2 - "Bye Bye Blackbird"
Sample 3 - "I'll Remember April"
Sample 4 - "The Lamp Is Low"
Sample 5 - "Just Friends"

Sample 1 - "Smile"

Sample 2 - "Bye Bye Blackbird"

Sample 3 - "I'll Remember April"

Sample 4 - "The Lamp is Low"

Sample 5 - "Just Friends"

Device reduction:

You may have noticed a variation on I-V-I in "Just Friends." It is possible to apply the same I-V-I device to the static harmony of only two measures by using three notes for each harmony instead of four. Outlining the I-V-I devices in segments of three beats still allows for a resolution to C on the downbeat of measure three after the two bars of C Major. This allows you to apply the same device to a static sound within a smaller space, without having to resolve to the original major tonality.

Example 5

Excerpt from "Just Friends"

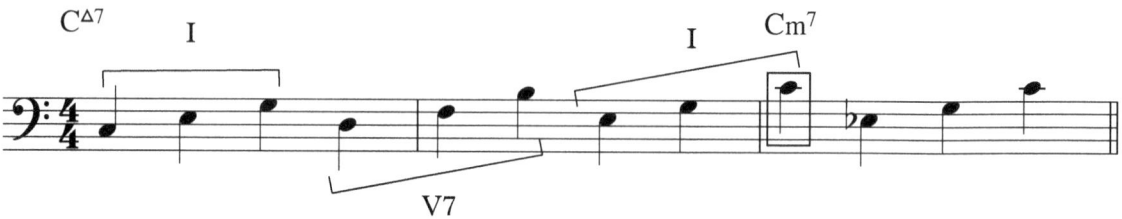

You must be thoughtful when using the I-V-I device over a two-measure static chord. If the third measure does not allow for natural resolution to a closely-related chord, the line would not work as well.

Adding tension with the V7b9 shape:

Until now, the I-V-I patterns have been limited to diatonic harmony. The examples so far have used a dominant shape starting on either chordal degree 5 (Shape A), or chordal degree 3 (Shape B) in the melody voice.

Example 6

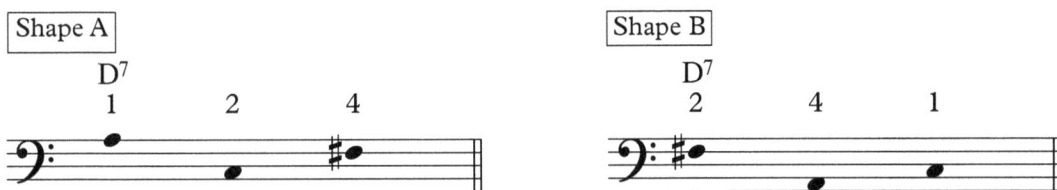

However, with the flexible nature of the dominant chord, a b9 can be implied using these shapes to create more tension and add color by starting on different chordal degrees. Adding the V7b9 to your vocabulary can further increase the hip factor in your bass lines. The I-V-I structures can now be sequenced both ascending and descending, allowing for travel around the bass with more freedom. You are no longer bound as strongly to any one position. With a dominant 7b9 chord, the core of the sound is a diminished chord.

"Smile" Excerpt

Bass line Sample 1 over "Smile" contained a b9 on the C7 chord in measure 14.

While this is a b9 over a dominant chord, this section deals only with V7b9 triadic shapes in the context of a I-V-I device.

Example 7a

D7b9 is really an F# Diminished 7 chord over D as the root. This relationship works for any dominant 7b9 chord.

Example 7b

Removing the 5th from the D7b9 (A) chord leaves F#, C, and Eb—the same fingering as Shape A. Though the 5th is missing, the chord still maintains its harmonic functionality.

Example 8a

Positioning dominant Shape A on scale degrees 3, 7, and b9 of any dominant chord will create a dominant 7b9 sound; starting on chordal degree 5 omits the b9.

Playing dominant Shape B on chordal degrees 5, 7, and b9 will also create a dominant 7b9 sound; starting on chordal degree 3 omits the b9.

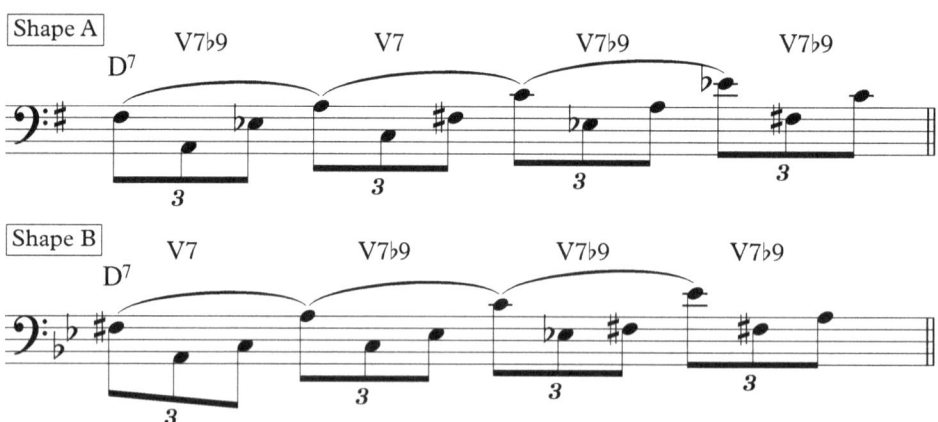

Shape A or B will work for any dominant chord when played beginning on chordal degrees 3, 5, 7, or b9.

The V7b9 shape is strongest from SD 4-to-3 or from b6-to-5 in the melody voice, as the natural tendency of the b9 to resolve downwards is emphasized most in these positions.

Exercises

Here are some basic applications of the ascending and descending 7b9 shapes. Like the dominant 7 shapes, they function the same in both major and minor tonalities.

Exercise 5a - ascending major

V7b9 ascending in F major using shapes A & B

Exercise 5b - descending major

V7b9 descending in F major using shapes A & B

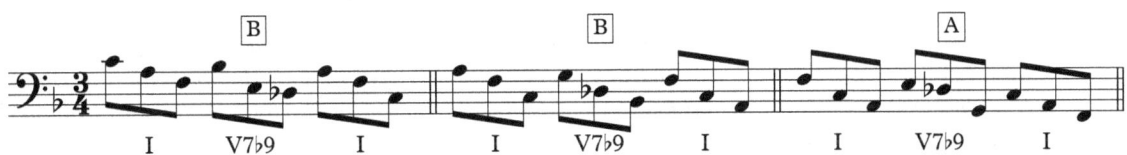

Exercise 6a - ascending minor

V7b9 ascending in F minor using shapes A & B

Exercise 6b - descending minor

V7b9 descending in F minor using shapes A & B

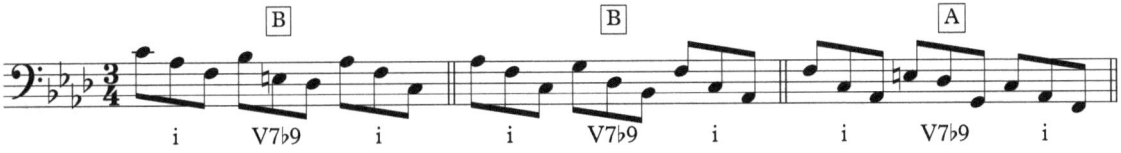

The two dominant 7b9 shapes are interchangeable. The best shape to choose will be governed by four factors: where you have just arrived from harmonically, where you are positionally, what's next in the form, and what is happening musically in the moment.

Using the V7b9 shapes in bass lines:

The following examples will revisit the same tunes used earlier. However, we will now use the dominant 7b9 shapes in place of the diatonic version, wherever possible.

Example 9

This example of "Bye Bye Blackbird" uses the dominant 7b9 in measures two and four.

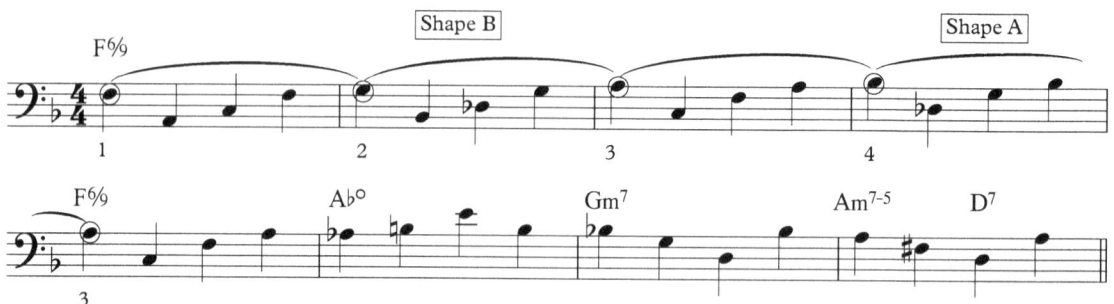

Example 10

This version of "Smile" uses the dominant 7b9 in measure two but I avoid it purposefully in measure four. Using the diatonic shape in measure four creates two clear independently descending lines (highlighted): G-F-Eb-D-Eb, and B-Bb-Ab-G. Using the dominant 7b9 in both measures would disrupt the natural downward flow of the line.

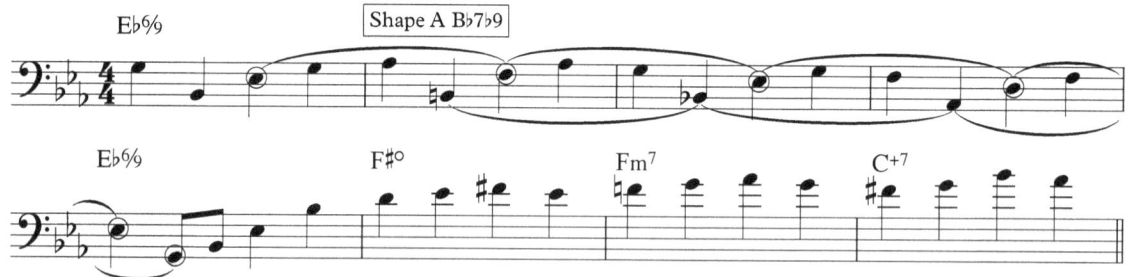

Example 11

This example of "I'll Remember April" uses both Shapes A and B to express the dominant 7b9 harmony.

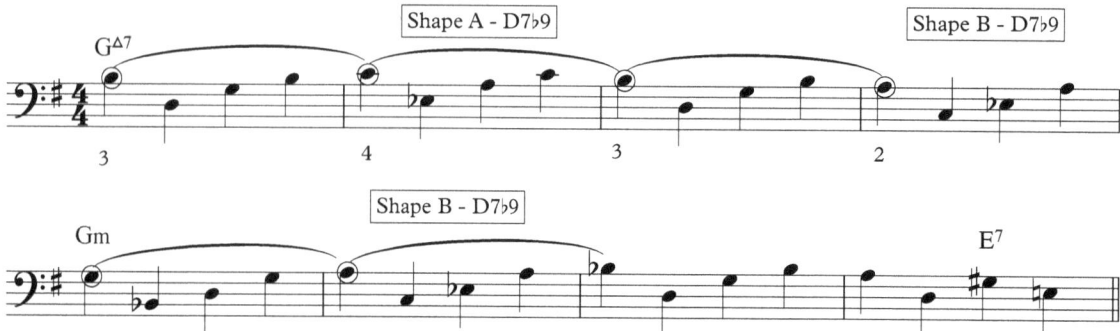

Breaking away from stationary patterns:

It is important to consider how to vary these patterns so they don't only occur in close proximity. All the patterns thus far travel no further than the closest appropriate neighboring shape. Being able to harmonize any tonic chord tone from any position is useful for understanding fingerboard layout, and is necessary for creating melodic walking bass lines. In the following examples, conceptualizing the top note as the melody note will greatly reinforce your ability to travel throughout the instrument.

Example 12

In this example, I have included scale degrees of the melody voice in the tonic key, G Major. See how quickly you can recognize the difference in Shapes A and B.

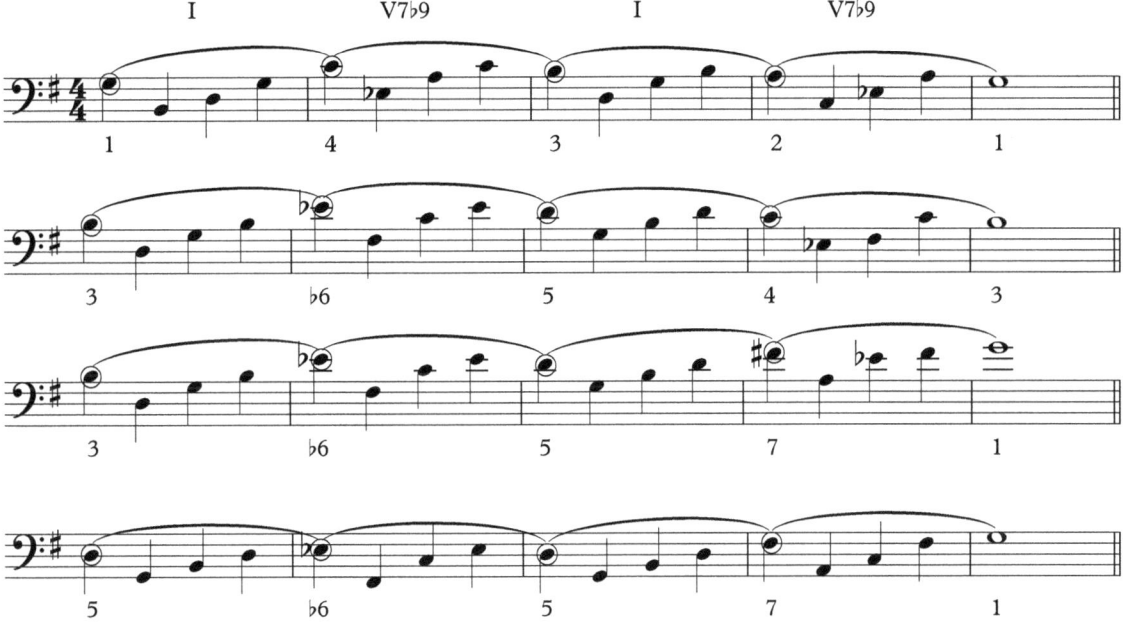

At this point, it is most beneficial to think about the scale degrees of your melodic voice movement in relation to the tonic. Only when the range becomes too low does it become advantageous to think of bass movement scale degrees.

Tonic-Dominant reference chart:

Reference the following charts to help understand the function (dominant or tonic) of each note in a key. Dominants function the same in both major and minor keys.

Example 13a - Major T-D Chart

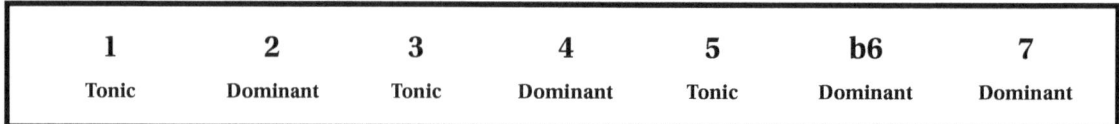

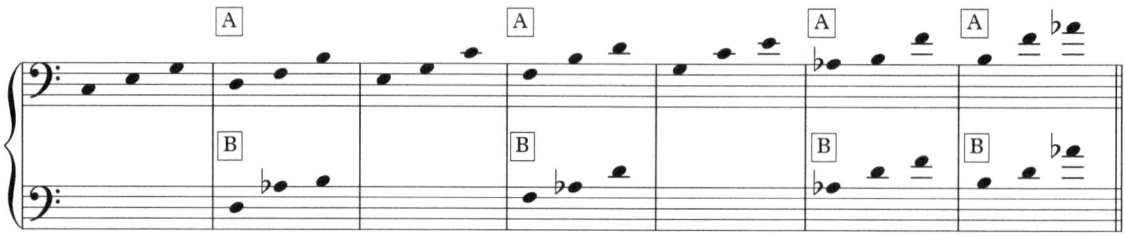

Example 13b - Minor T-D Chart

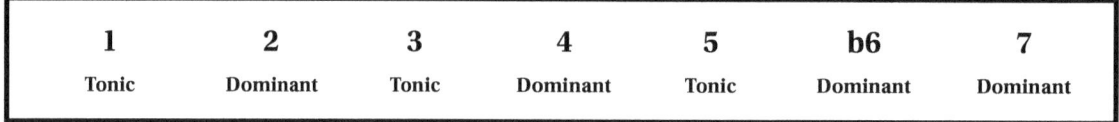

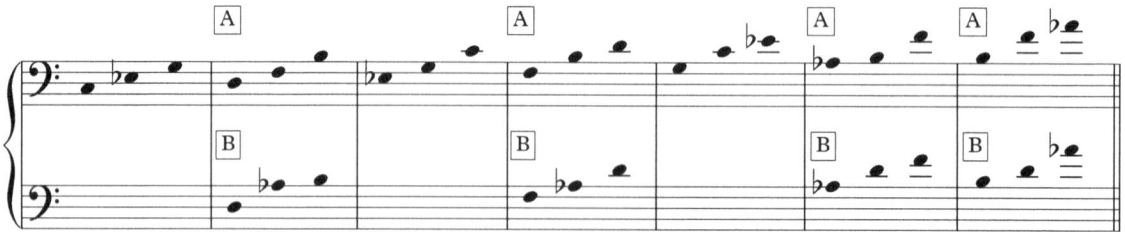

Final thoughts

The best use of this material is with a variety of other walking material. The I-V-I device alone, however, can significantly strengthen your understanding of harmony. Using this system to assign tonic and dominant labels to every note means that every sound you hear, choice you make, and way you think about interacting will be fundamentally rooted in strong, stable, and supportive harmony.

Sample bass lines

I've included sample bass lines that use these principles when possible. Transcribing great bassists, listening to recordings, learning melodies, and writing bass lines are all important pieces of the learning puzzle. These samples highlight the I-V-I device over static harmony, mixed with more conventional vocabulary (scalar based movement, chromaticism to roots, and linear target notes). Minimal analysis is included other than where the instances of I-V-I are used. Assume that these bass lines occur behind solo lines, not the melody.

Sample 6 - "Smile"

Sample 7 - "Bye Bye Blackbird"

Sample 8 - "I'll Remember April"

Sample 9 - "The Lamp Is Low"

Sample 10 - "Just Friends"

Sample 6 - "Smile"

Sample 7 - "Bye Bye Blackbird"

Chorus 2

Chorus 3

Sample 8 - "I'll Remember April"

Sample 9 - "The Lamp Is Low"

Chorus 1

Sample 10 - "Just Friends"

Chorus 3

Chapter 2

Adapting I-V-I to Harmony of
Two Bars Length

Chapter 2

In Chapter 1, I introduced the I-V-I device using static chords with a length of three or more bars. In several instances, I manipulated the rhythmic content to fit a span of two bars. Those examples only worked in specific situations and required truncating the concept to three notes per implied harmony (tonic & dominant) to make it fit. It is still easiest to convey the I-V-I relationship over a length of at least three bars, as it provides adequate time to resolve each function with four notes per bar. It is possible, though, to express the same I-V-I functionality in static harmony of two bars. A minimum of six beats is needed in any time signature—not just 4/4—in order to fulfill the voice leading. Condensing the I-V-I device to two bars increases harmonic rhythm while simultaneously simplifying the nature of the sound. This is in contrast to Reduction Harmony (introduced in Chapter 4), which slows down the perceived harmonic rhythm.

The shortest bar length over which you can convey the I-V-I relationship is two bars of a static chord, and requires expressing each function with only two notes instead of four. In a space of eight beats, this represents two beats each for tonic, dominant, and then tonic before moving on to other harmonies in the line. When only using two notes, the 6th is the strongest interval to outline harmony. It can express movement of simple diatonic through advanced chromatic harmony, ii-V-I's with alterations, etc. The I-V-I device, when played over two bars, is represented by intervals of a 6th and can outline the most pertinent notes for clear voice leading, including upper extensions.

The 6th is not only an incredibly powerful interval on the bass, but plays a significant role in Western Harmony. The simplest and most effective way to harmonize a sound is with 6ths and then 3rds. On the bass, the space of a 3rd provides less resonance than a 6th. A 10th, while most resonant, requires quite a bit of distance between strings to execute, so playing a 6th minimizes the physical distance (always one string unless starting on an open string) while creating maximum resonance. Besides the advantage of sound, use of 6ths allows bass players to organize their bass lines into two independent moving voices in motion, conceiving the bass function as one of multi-voice counterpoint.

Condensing 3 note shapes to 2:

To find these intervals, we will revisit triadic I-V-I structure and isolate the outside notes. These "shells" provide harmonic clarity and facilitate movement. Though you will play both notes in succession while walking, knowing how they function vertically is what solidifies your understanding of this concept. This concept functions similarly in both major and minor.

Example 1a - Bb Major

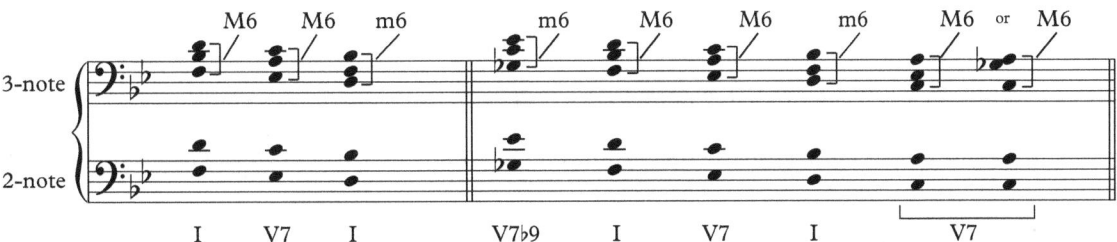

Example 1b - Bb Minor

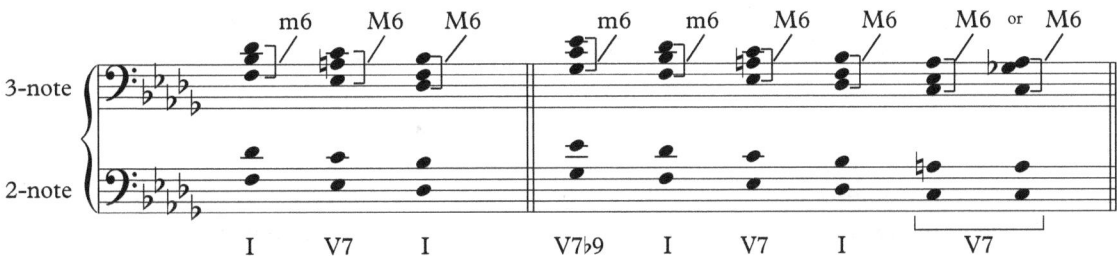

Understanding the 6th in practice:

If you look for them, you will see 6ths embedded in the internal structure of all chords. In Example 2, I have extracted all the 6ths from within a ii-V-I by looking for any 6th that exists between chord tones. Thinking about chords as the sum of their intervals gives voice leading and sequencing many more possibilities. The examples to follow will demonstrate some of the possibilities using 6ths.

Example 2 - ii-V-I

F# to Eb is technically a diminished 7th, but it fits the same handshape as if it were a 6th.

Example 3 - "Have You Met Miss Jones" (Bridge)

In this example, I use 6ths to outline the ii-V-I movement in the bridge:

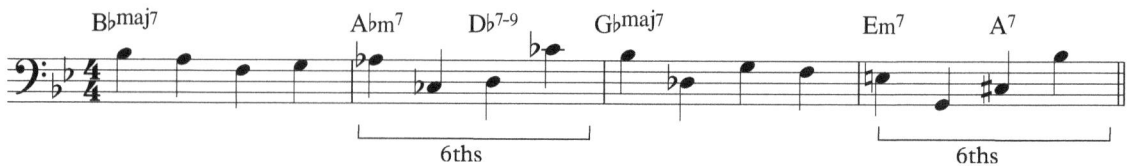

Example 4 - "Stella By Starlight" (Bridge)

In this example, I use 6ths to outline a variety of harmonies: altered dominant sounds over G7, a i-V-i device over C Minor 11, lydian dominant over Ab7#11, and a I-V-I device over the Bb Major 7. This demonstrates how to effectively create melodic continuity in a walking bass line using primarily 6ths.

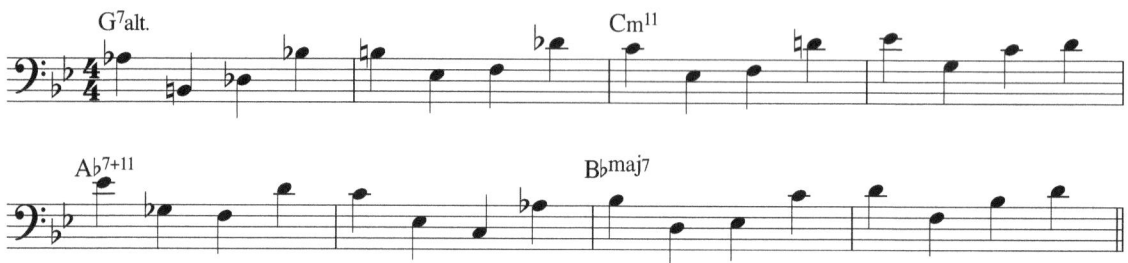

Examples 4 and 5 represent some of the many possibilities when using 6ths in a walking bass line. For the purpose of the chapter, we will focus on expressing I-V-I motion within a static major or minor harmony of two bars length.

Exercises

Using it in walking:

Here are some basic applications of the ascending and descending 7b9 shapes. Like the dominant 7 shapes, they function the same in both major and minor tonalities.

Example 5a - Major

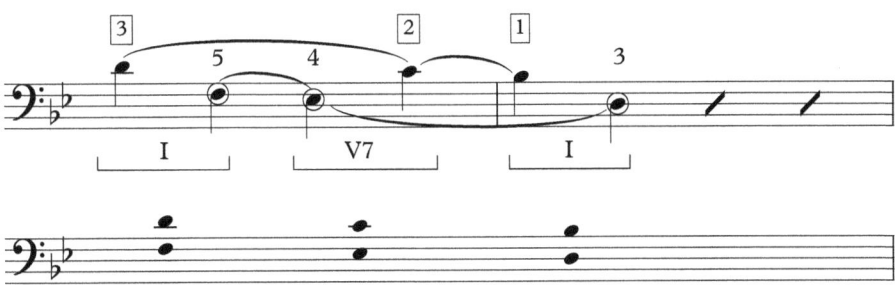

Example 5b - minor

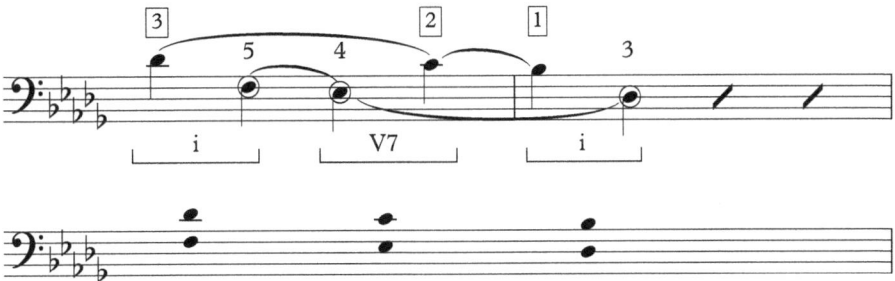

As a reminder, the same paradigms from the previous chapter will form the foundation for the following exercises:

Example 5c

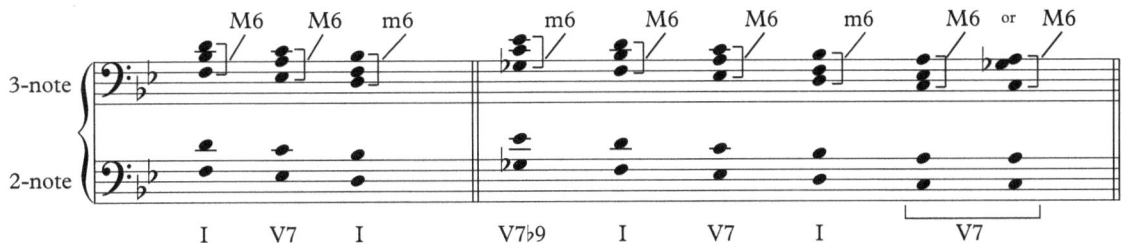

Exercise 1 - I-V-I in Major

This exercise demonstrates the I-V-I in 12 major keys, following a melody motion of 3-4-3-2-1. Note the use of V7b9 with SD 4 in the melody note.

Exercise 2 - Basic i-V-i in Minor

This exercise demonstrates the i-V-i in 12 minor keys, with a melody motion of 3-4-3-2-1.

Exercise 3 - Switching Between Tonalities

This exercise uses the V7 shape to switch between major and minor tonalities. Find more than one fingering solution to execute these devices.

Exercise 4 - Moving Through Different Keys

The 6th facilitates movement between keys. This exercise moves from I to IV to I, using a 7b9 to pivot between keys. This harmonic movement is particularly useful in the blues, which will be demonstrated in Example 7.

Example 6a - Bb Blues (Major)

Example 6a uses a major I-V-I device in measures three and five of the blues, and minor in measure 9. Using I-V-I in these instances provides an effective alternative to the scale approach when outlining tonic sounds. Look for examples in both major and minor tonalities, and take notice of the V7b9 shape in measure 4 that pivots to the IV chord.

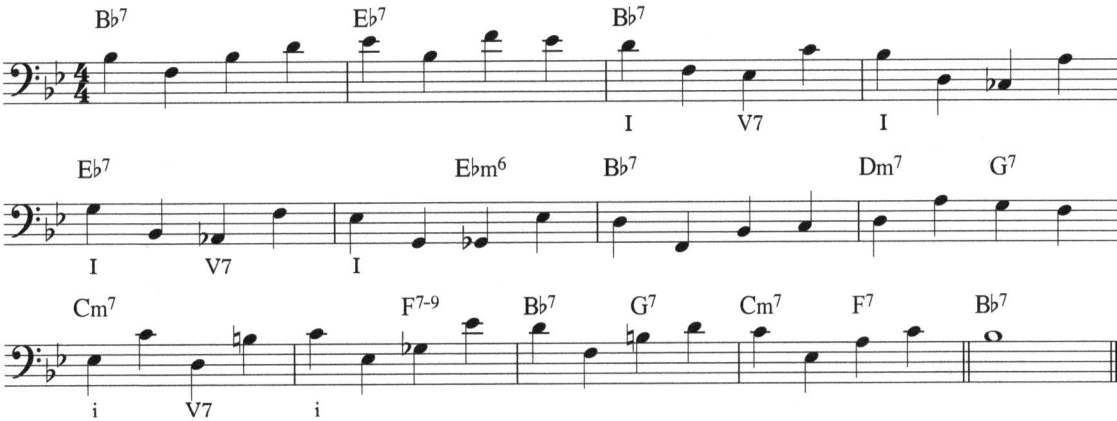

Example 6b - Bb Blues (Minor)

Example 7b uses a minor i-V-i device in measures three and five of the blues. The devices are equally as effective in both major and minor tonalities.

Traveling I-V-I patterns:

There is only one I-V-I device that can be played in close proximity without resolving to the same tonic chord: melody motion 3-2-1 or 1-2-3.

Example 7 - Linear

7a - Descending 3-2-1 in melody voice

7b - Ascending 1-2-3 in melody voice

All other executions of the device in close proximity begin and end on the same tonic chord:

Example 8 - Neighbor

8a - Upper neighbor tone on V

8b - Lower neighbor tone on V

To increase melodicism in the bass lines, it is imperative to break out of the positional nature of these devices. By traveling the melody note throughout the full range of the instrument, your melodic possibilities increase as you are no longer reliant on resolving in the same position.

It helps to think of the melody note when conceptualizing traveling. The following examples travel to non-neighboring melody notes in order to complete the resolution. The first example express 3-7-1 in the melody voice; the second example express 1-4-3 in the melody voice.

Example 9 - Traveling (non-linear)

9a - Descending fourth in melody

9b - Ascending fourth in melody

The process for creating lines with this technique is straightforward: Pick a tonic melody note (1 or 3), and then a V-I resolution (7-1, 2-3, 4-3). Breaking the device in two parts facilitates easier travel throughout the instrument.

Exercise 5

This exercise represents some traveling options in major and minor tonalities. See what melody motion you can recognize. The melody motion does not always fall on beat 1.

Sample Bass Lines

The core mission of Chapter II is to add functionality and strengthen harmonic understanding in walking bass. As with the Chapter I, the samples in this chapter contain only quarter notes, as a solid bass line needs little more than a focused sound, clear harmony, and strong pulse.

I-V-I in two measures:

Here are some 8-bar examples that apply the I-V-I device to two measures of static major or minor chords. The I-V-I device is typically only used over major and minor tonic chords, though in cases like the blues where the dominant chord functions as tonic, this is totally acceptable.

> Sample 1 - "There Will Never Be Another You"
> Sample 2 - "Just Friends"
> Sample 3 - "Take the 'A' Train"
> Sample 4 - "How High the Moon"
> Sample 5 - "On a Clear Day"
> Sample 6 - "East of the Sun"
> Sample 7 - "G Blues"

Traveling I-V-I patterns:

These samples represent both traveling and neighboring I-V-I patterns. The dominant 7b9 shape and diatonic shapes are both used.

> Sample 8 - "There Will Never Be Another You"
> Sample 9 - "Smile"
> Sample 10 - "The Lamp Is Low"
> Sample 11 - "Alone Together (Bridge)"
> Sample 12 - "I'll Be Seeing You" (B Section)
> Sample 13 - "Autumn Leaves"
> Sample 14 - "All Or Nothing At All"

I-V-I in two measures:

Sample 1 - "There Will Never Be Another You"

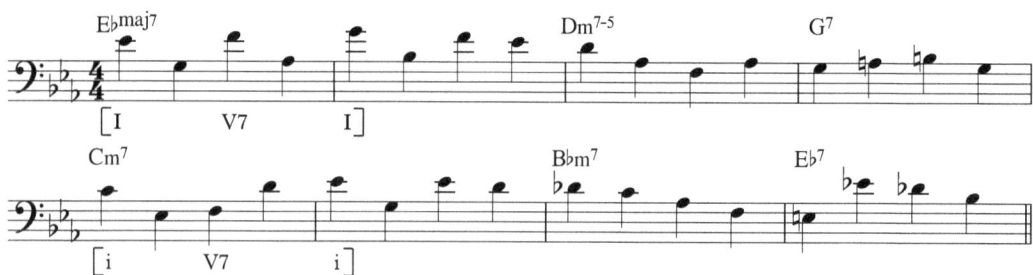

Sample 2 - "Just Friends"

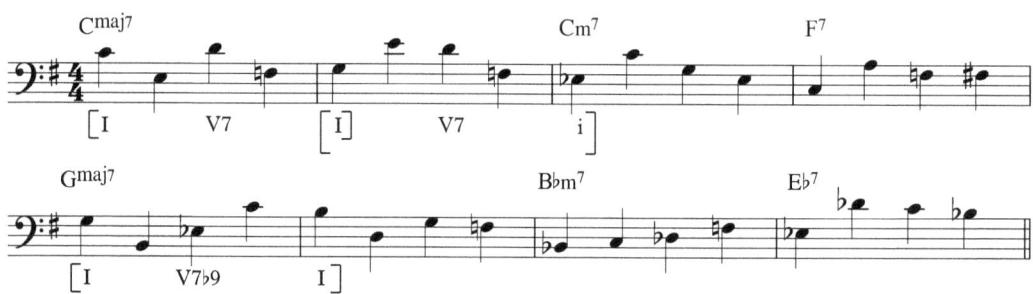

Sample 3 - "Take the 'A' Train"

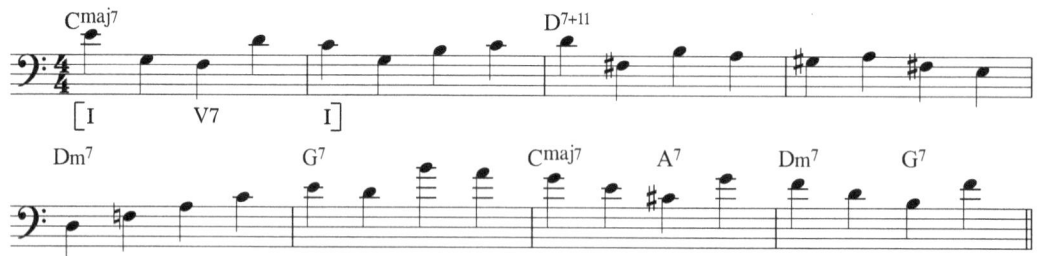

Sample 4 - "How High the Moon"

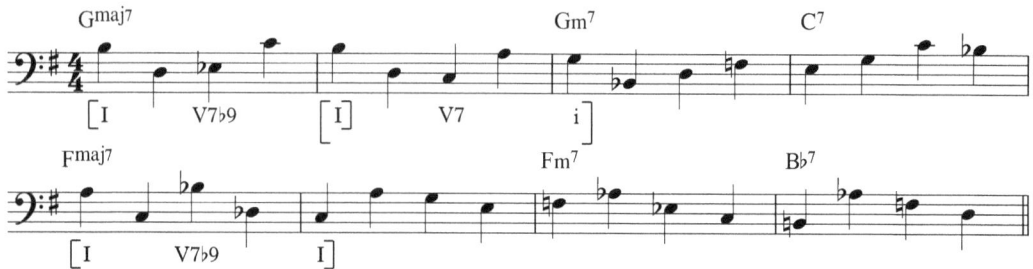

Sample 5 - "On a Clear Day"

Sample 6 - "East of the Sun"

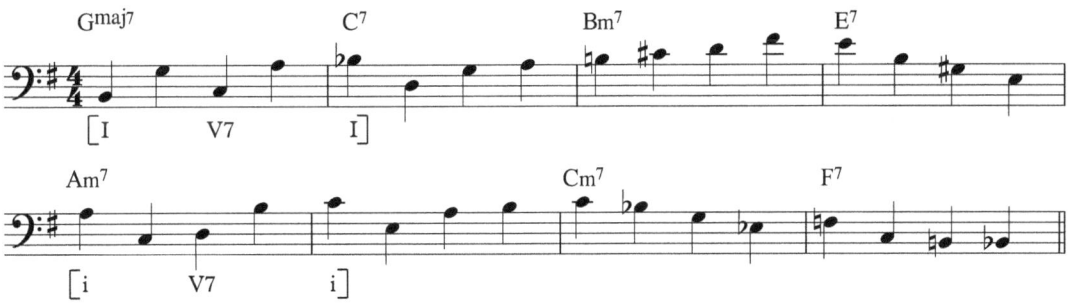

Sample 7 - G Blues

Traveling I-V-I patterns:

Sample 8 - "There Will Never Be Another You"

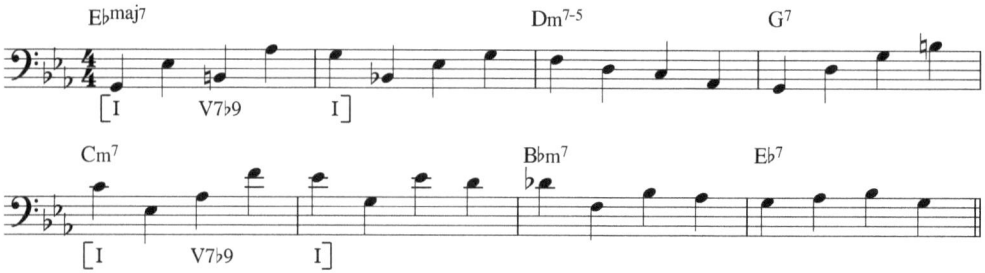

Sample 9 - "Smile"

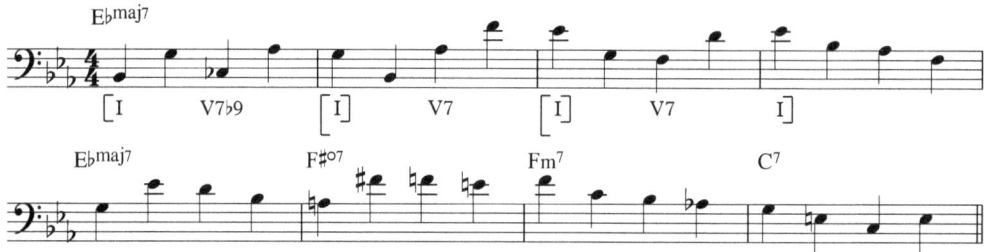

Sample 10 - "The Lamp Is Low"

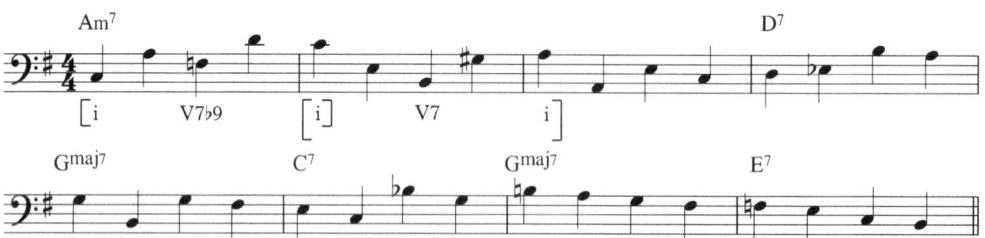

Sample 11 - "Alone Together" (Bridge)

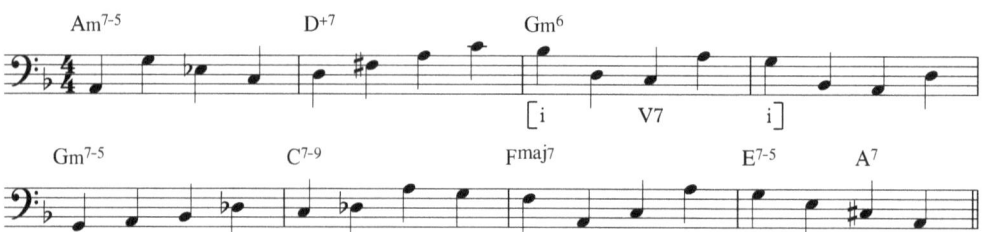

Sample 12 - "I'll Be Seeing You" (B Section)

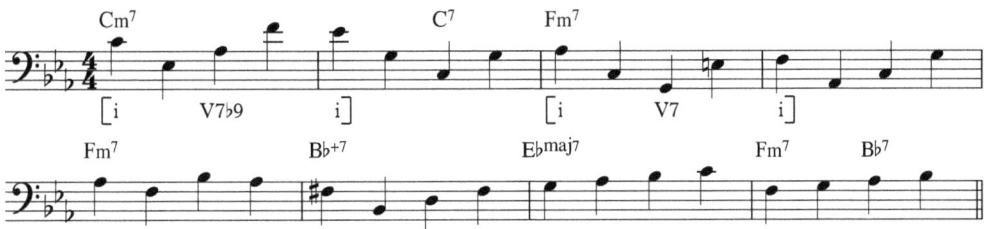

Sample 13 - "Autumn Leaves"

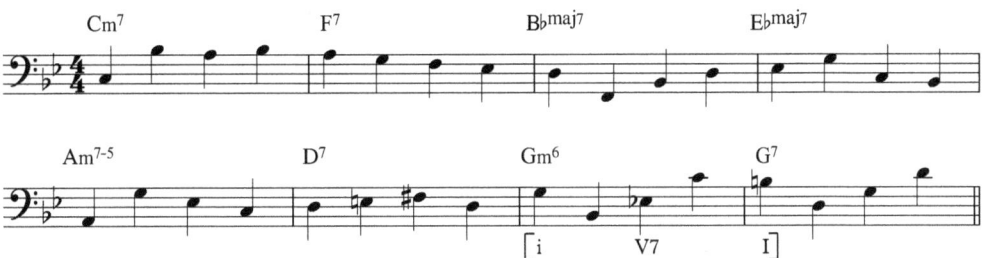

Sample 14 - "All Or Nothing At All"

Full Samples

Here are more sample bass lines that incorporate the I-V-I device on static chords. These samples demonstrate how to use this idea in conjunction with other typical bass line vocabulary. Harmonic analysis has intentionally been omitted. Look for examples of the I-V-I (or i-V-i) device and use of 6ths to outline implied harmonies.

Sample 15 - "On a Clear Day"
Sample 16 - "Bb Blues"
Sample 17 - "Cherokee"

Sample 15 - "On a Clear Day"

Sample 16 - "Bb Blues"

Sample 17 - "Cherokee"

Chorus 2

Chapter 3

Triadic ii-V-I Shapes

Chapter 3

The choices we make when walking bass lines in a group setting are influenced by a number of variables: the fixed harmony at that given moment, what the other musicians are doing, and how fast we can react to it. In addition to responding and adjusting accordingly to what is happening in the moment, it is our job to anticipate where the music is going before we get there. Unfortunately, the nature of the bass allows us to hide behind our harmonic limitations unlike any other instrument. This can make it difficult to reach our full musical potential. Even further, it can be easy to lose clarity while balancing our many responsibilities. This is especially true as we want to free the music, and it is even more difficult in a straight-ahead context. We may struggle to react appropriately while maintaining harmonic support without abandoning ii-V-I progressions entirely.

This chapter explains the implied harmony above and below a chord in a ii-V-I progression, even in situations where the harmony is not directly articulated. Similar to the I-V-I studies in Chapter 1, knowing the implications of each note choice will lead to the most supportive bass functions. This method of organization will heighten your awareness of how each note functions in a ii-V-I progression. These walking bass line studies focus on ii-V-I progressions with one chord per measure, using basic chord tones and the V7b9 chord. Many of these shapes are borrowed from the I-V-I harmony in Chapter 1.

Guitarists and pianists are aware of multiple moving harmonies simultaneously while comping. The nature of their instruments force them to use appropriate voice leading, which may vary by situation, but bassists get by walking only one note at a time. Comping instruments are able to address ii-V-I voice leading through many different colors: drop 2 voicings; 4, 5, and 6 note voicings; extensions; quartal harmony; etc. This is all influenced by what is happening in the moment. The studies in this chapter will help you generate walking bass line content that is melodic yet fundamentally solid, favoring intervals that move in linear motion. Think of these studies as studies in arpeggiated comping. They are immediately applicable and will vastly deepen your understanding of fingerboard harmony and remove the ambiguity in your playing.

The inherent limitations of playing double bass usually preclude us from adopting harmony practices similar to other instrumentalists. While single-note instrumentalists cannot express multiple notes at once, instruments which are more naturally dexterous—saxophone and trumpet for example—can express wide intervals and navigate octave leaps quickly with ease, creating an effect similar to polyphony. Compared to the distance a bassist must traverse in order to express something similar, it's impractical. Though some bassists reach the level of virtuosity needed to express these ideas, the majority won't—nor do they need to. These exercise simplify the concept by addressing multiple lines of voice leading in a walking context.

The goals of practicing these ii-V-I patterns are to:

1. Simplify the way one interacts with ii-V-I's, increasing melodic sensibilities
2. Learn how ii-V-I's function throughout the whole fingerboard
3. Break dependence on relating harmony to the root of a chord
4. Visualize multiple lines of harmony moving at once
5. Interact more meaningfully with comping instruments and the soloist

To provide a strong bass foundation, it is necessary to understand the basics of four-note voice leading, and how comping instrumentalists fundamentally conceive of harmonic movement. With this knowledge, you will be able to better support solo lines without clashing with chordal players.

Basics of four-note voice leading:

Example 1

Example 1 shows a basic chordal execution of a ii-V-I in root position (each chord is arpeggiated above the root).

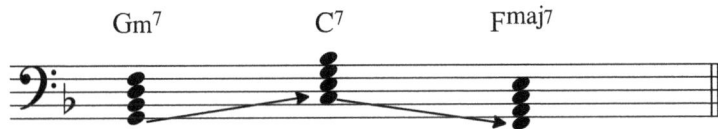

Though theoretically clear, harmony that moves from root position chords is extremely inefficient—each voice jumps too far. Smooth voice leading favors movement of a half step or whole step between voices. Most comping instrumentalists invert or reorder their chord voicings to make this possible.

Example 2

Example 2 represents how a comping instrumentalist may address inversions of a basic seventh chord in a ii-V-I.

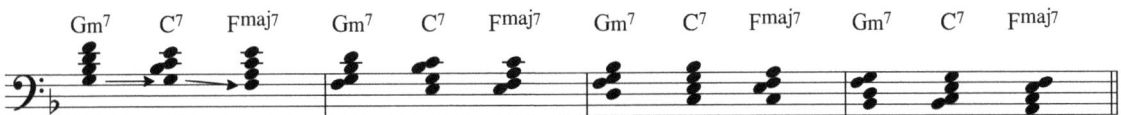

Not every voice has to move, allowing for the smoothest possible voice leading. If a note does move, it moves a maximum of a whole step. Notice how the top note of each chord forms a melody over the four bar progression.

Example 3

The same rules apply to voice leading in minor. Notice how the dominant shape functions similarly in major and minor.

Though bass players only express one note a time in a walking line—not multiple notes like a comping instrument—it is impractical to conceptualize harmony as moving from one root position chord to the next root position chord. Bassists are the only instrumentalists who exclusively outline root movement, which may be why it is quite difficult to conceptualize harmony without the root of the chord. Having access to harmony from any position on the bass reduces our dependence on the root.

**A chord played in context does not need the root
in order be interpreted as that sound.**

Examples 1, 2, and 3 used only chord tones for the sake of clarity, but practical comping situations differ slightly from the previous examples in two ways. First, comping instruments generally disregard the root and instead incorporate more colorful notes.

Example 4a

This example replaces the root on Gm7 with a 9th (A), and the root of C7 with a b9 (Db), creating more colorful moving harmony.

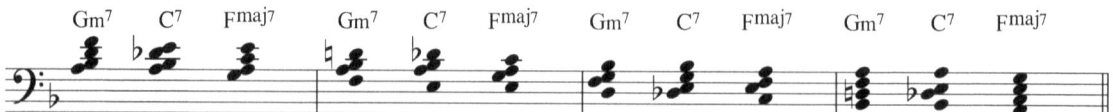

Secondly, comping instruments don't always favor dense voicings. The voicings in Example 4a are called closed voicings; the notes and movement all occur in close proximity.

Example 4b

This example (taken from the second measure in Example 4a) is called a Drop-2 voicing; the second voice from the top of an arpeggio (Gm7: F-A-Bb-D) is "dropped" down one octave (Bb-F-A-D). It allows for more distance between notes, reducing the density of the voicing. It also presents a clearer visual representation of the independent lines voice leading.

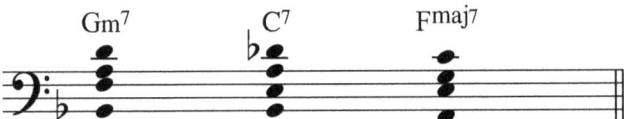

Exercise 5 contains a 12-key major workout of drop-2 arpeggios.

Again, a chord doesn't have to be arpeggiated from root position, nor does it need to contain the root to be identifiable. So, what does this mean for us, and how can we apply it to our walking patterns?

Adapting voice leading for bassists:

Applying voice leading principles to the bass requires condensing the four-note chord shapes into three-note shapes. Though four notes will be notated in every measure, one pitch will be repeated. The discussion will be divided into two parts: descending and ascending chord shapes. The most appropriate three notes will be chosen depending on what is available in any given position, out of the four available positions. They will also change depending on whether you are ascending or descending the ii-V-I patterns, in minor, etc.

When applying the shapes, keep the following in mind:

1. The shapes are organized starting with the ii chord
2. The patterns occur from any starting pitch within the ii chord: 1, b3, 5, b7
3. You will only use three notes to express each chord quality

Example 5

The voicings in this example will form the foundation for what notes are used in the rest of this chapter. The V7b9 shape (from Chapter 2) will be applied freely over dominant chords to incorporate the most colorful notes as often as possible.

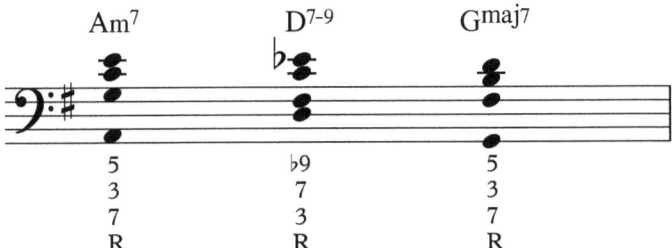

Descending chord sequences: Major:

Descending sequences provide considerably different choices than ascending sequences. The natural tendency of the V7 chord, particularly with a b9, is to resolve downwards. This brings more weight to your descending bass lines. Using the V7b9 chord in descending sequences provides more note choices for your ii and V chords, and the core of your line will be reinforced by a strong dominant shape.

Example 6

Here is the full collection of descending ii-V-I patterns, beginning from the 5th of the ii chord. This pattern can start from any pitch in the ii chord, though your choice of patterns will be governed by range: starting on E in the melody voice (the 5th of Am7) allows for a comfortable descent through all the patterns without running out of fingerboard space. The descending patterns are labeled based on the melody voice (or top note) of the ii chord.

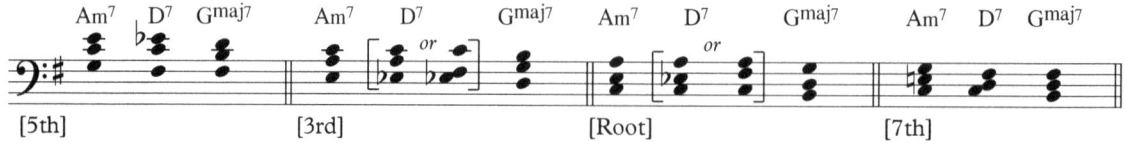

Tip: Think of the starting notes in relation to the ii chord and the overall key

From the 5th of the ii chord:

In this position, the root is not present in any of the chords. The gravity of the 7b9 shape is strong enough to provide the perception of a complete resolution, even without the root.

Example 7a

Example 7b

Example 7a applied in a walking pattern looks like this. Though there are four notes in each measure, the first pitch of each three-note pattern is repeated.

From the 3rd of the ii chord:

This position provides root movement as an inner voice. The 7b9 can shape can be utilized two ways, though the first shape comes easier as there is no shifting involved.

Example 8a

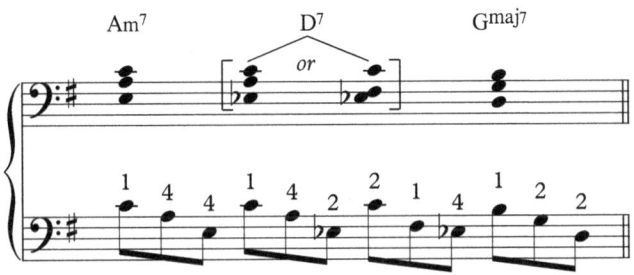

Example 8b

Example 8a applied in a walking pattern looks like this. Notice the three-note patterns repeat the first pitch.

In the second measure, placing C on beat 1 of D7 creates repeated notes and results in a weaker line. Repeated notes are a necessary vocabulary in walking bass lines, but usually occur in even pairings—beats 1 & 2 or beats 3 & 4—not over the barline as in this example.

Example 8c

This example addresses the repeated note problem from Example 8b. Chords that reuse the same top note may need to be re-arpeggiated to maintain smooth voice leading.

From the Root of the ii chord:

This example provides the most "bass" functionality—the root is articulated on the downbeat of the Am7 and GMaj7 chord, though not in the bass voice.

Example 9a

Harmonically, this progression functions as Am—Adim—GMaj7. Example 9b demonstrates that, depending on how you view the roots, it could also be CMaj6—Cm6—GMaj7

Example 9b

Diminished ii° functions as a dominant, and is indicative of an older harmonic sound. Minor iv can always be used as a dominant chord, and you'll find that it presents you with more melodic options when coming from a ii chord. The last four bars of "I'll Be Seeing You", for example, can interchange the functions of ii° and iv depending on whether one is supporting the melody or a soloist.

Example 9c

Here is a realization of Example 9a in a walking context. Notice how the root of the Am7 and GMaj7 chords is still on the downbeat, though not in the bass voice.

From the 7th of the ii chord:

This example is the least supportive choice for your bass lines, though still beneficial to know. The range forces the voice leading down to the lower register of the bass. This would be acceptable if it emphasized root notes, but placing 3rds and 7ths in the melody voice can contribute muddiness to the overall sound. More importantly, as the tonic is G, emphasizing G on the downbeat of Amin7 can sound like a mistake and create doubt in the harmony.

Example 10a

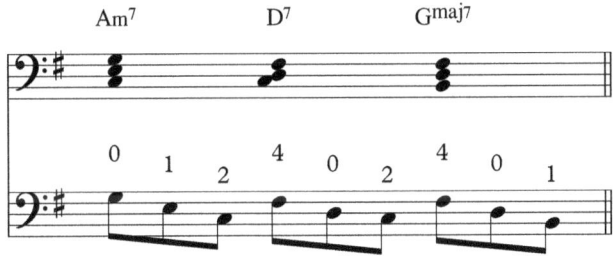

SD 1-7-7 of the tonic

Example 10b

A fully realized bass line in a walking context would look like this. The notes in measure three have been reordered to avoid doubling F# on beats four and one.

Exercises

Using descending ii-V-I's in walking situations:

Here are the same patterns realized in a walking context, progressing through the collection of ii-V-I chords from Example 6. Inserting these patterns into walking bass lines is quite easy. Wherever there is a major ii-V-I of one bar per chord, you can incorporate one of these descending patterns.
Practice with a metronome at a variety of tempos to solidify the movement underneath your fingers. For further practice, transpose the exercises into distantly related keys.

Exercise 1

Further Practice: Adding the VI chord:

Introducing the VI chord allows you to string all four descending major patterns together. The ii-V-I-VI progression is a staple in numerous jazz standards, as well a common tag to end tunes. In Exercise 1, each line ends with two measure of the tonic (I) chord. In Exercise 2, one measure of tonic will now be followed by one measure of the VI chord. The move from VI to ii is simply just a minor V7-i relationship.

Exercise 2

The V7 shape, introduced in Chapter 1, will represent either V7 or V7b9 functionality. The cyclical nature of this pattern allows these patterns to be performed without stopping.

Moving the last sequence up on octave (by reordering the notes of E7 in measure 11) allows for a smooth repeat back to the top of the form. Feel free to use shape A or shape B from Chapter 1 for the V7 in the third line, if you would like to create more tension with a b9.

Once you become familiar with the exercise, begin to experiment with incorporating other walking bass vocabulary. Try staying down an octave for the last line (including the E7 in measure 11) and finding your own way back up to the top of the exercise. Try different shapes for the V7 chords.

Exercise 3

I strongly recommend applying these new concepts over "Autumn Leaves" because this tune offers myriad opportunities to practice ii-Vs in context. It also allows you to sequence patterns in both major and minor tonalities, which will be taught in later sections.

In addition to reading these lines, practice writing your own. Here are a few ways to adapt this bass line for your own practice:

- Read four bars and then improvise the next four bars with related or contrasting ideas
- Practice each line starting on a different chordal degree
- Start in thumb position and descend your line to the lowest register available
- Practice this in unfamiliar position the bass
- Write a new bass line in a different key using the same shapes

Exercise 4 - All the Things You Are

Here's another example using "All the Things You Are." Notice the first application (beginning in measure 2) starts on chordal degree 3 as in Example 8c, and the second application (beginning in measure 10) starts on chordal degree 1 as in Example 9c.

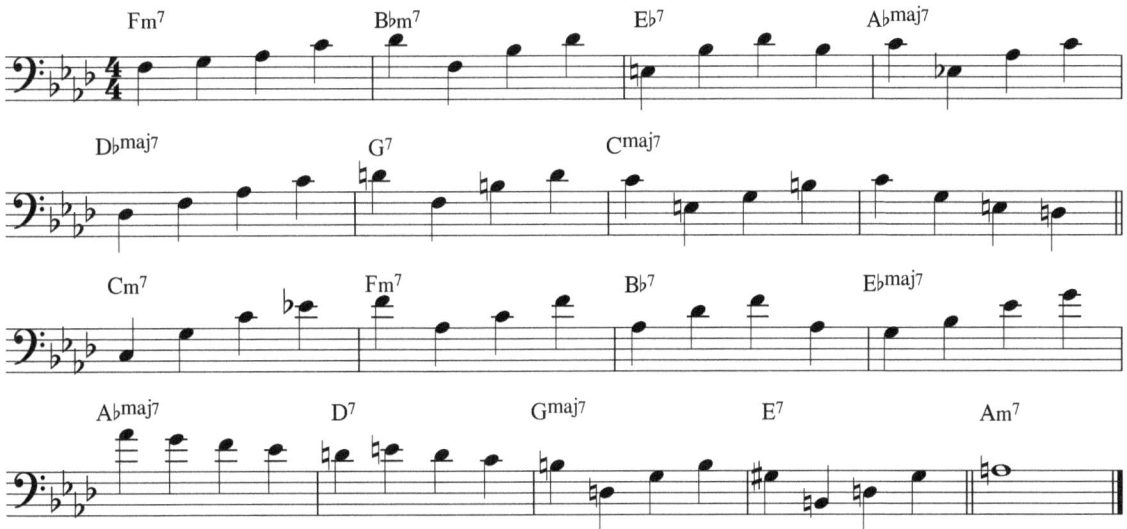

In addition to reading these lines, practice writing your own. Here are a few ways to adapt this bass line for your own practice:

- Read four bars and then improvise the next four bars with related or contrasting ideas
- Practice each line starting on a different chordal degree
- Start in thumb position and descend your line to the lowest register available
- Practice this in unfamiliar position the bass
- Write a new bass line in a different key using the same shapes

Exercise 5 - ii-V-I-VI Drop-2 arpeggios

These exercises deviate from the triadic shape, arpeggiating ii-V-I's using the drop 2 method described earlier in this chapter. These are all rootless voicing. Some patterns may need to be adjusted for the octave; your comfort level on the instrument will govern what you transpose. For further practice, try adapting this exercise to minor keys.

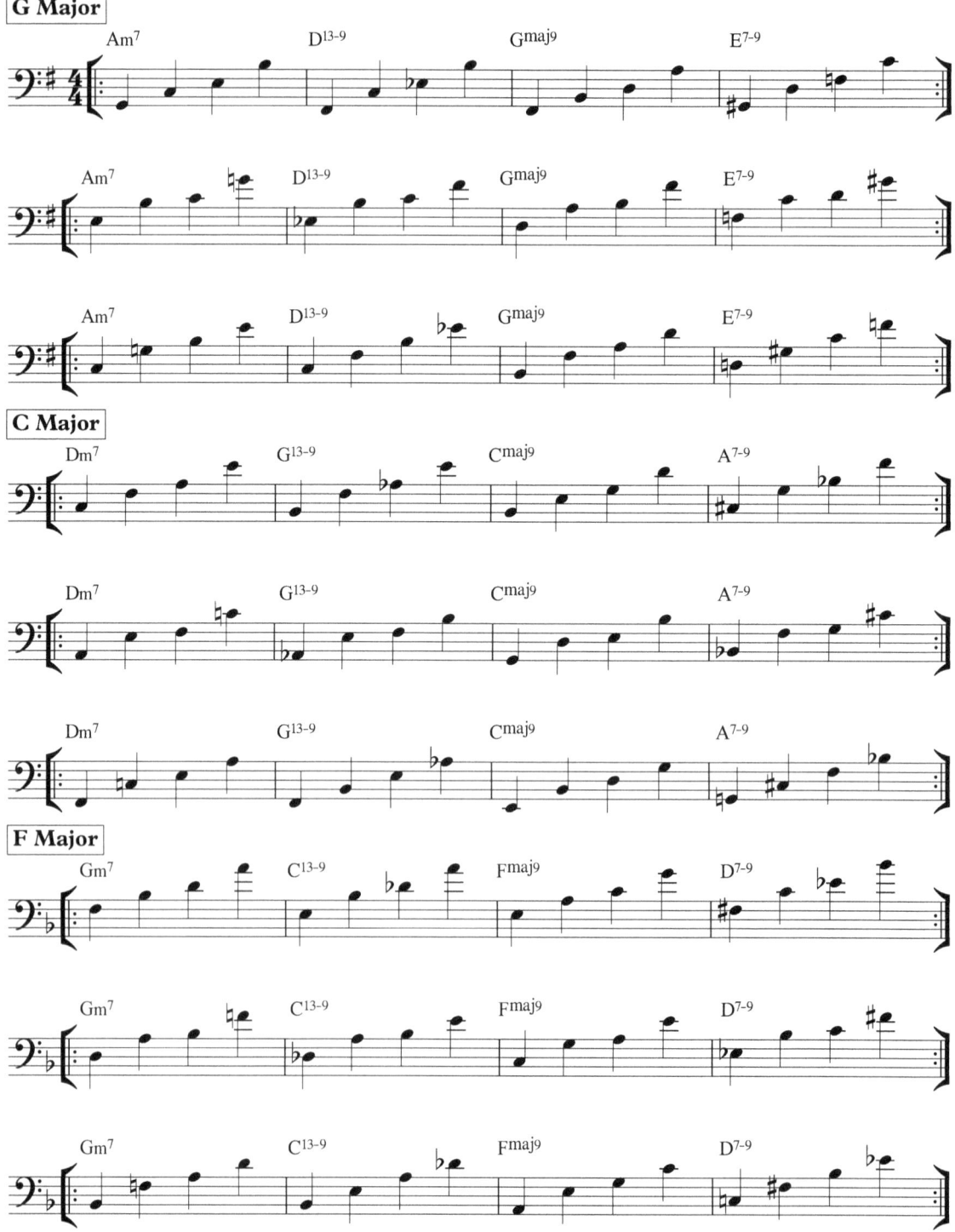

Descending chord sequences: Minor:

In this section, minor ii-V-i progressions are grouped by position, following the same procedure as in major keys, with positions organized by the starting pitch of the ii chord. You can walk over a minor and major ii-V-I progression with the same triadic texture; the differences in a walking context are minimal. Other than the change in predominant—minor to diminished—the application of the V7 chord remains the same, as well as the projected resolution to tonic.

Example 13

These notes inform what shapes are used in a minor key:

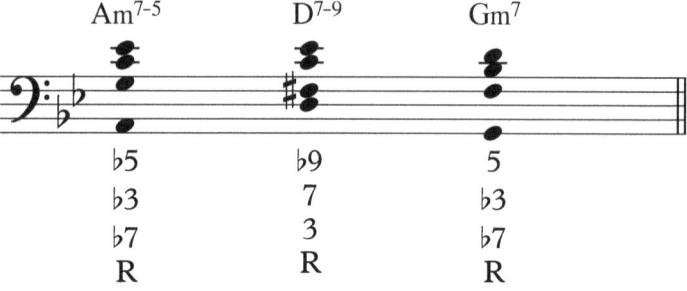

Though quite similar, the use of ii° presents one unique challenge which must be addressed with care. Remember, the core structure of dominant shapes A & B (Chapter 1, Example 6) is diminished, and the starting pitch determines whether the chord is diatonic or b9.

Example 14a

D7b9 is really an F# Diminished 7 chord over D as the root. It is reduced to three notes in example 14b.

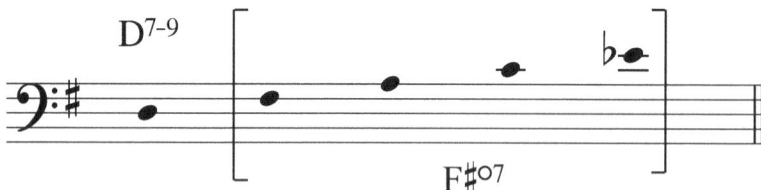

Example 14b

As the predominant in minor is diminished, the core triadic shape of the predominant and dominant is the same.

Example 15

This is an example of ii-V-I progressions in parallel major and minor. The Am7b5 chord and D7b9 use exactly the same notes, yet they offer very different functions.

If we were to use the D7b9 in the key of G Minor, the same shape would be used for both the predominant and dominant. There would appear to be no harmonic movement between the chords, and nothing would indicate strong movement to the tonic. Therefore when expressing a minor ii°-V-i progression, the predominant shape will determine which dominant shape to use.

Example 16

You may recognize this from Exercise 3. This example shows a practical situation in which the problem discussed in Example 15 is avoided by using Shape B for the ii°-V in a minor key.

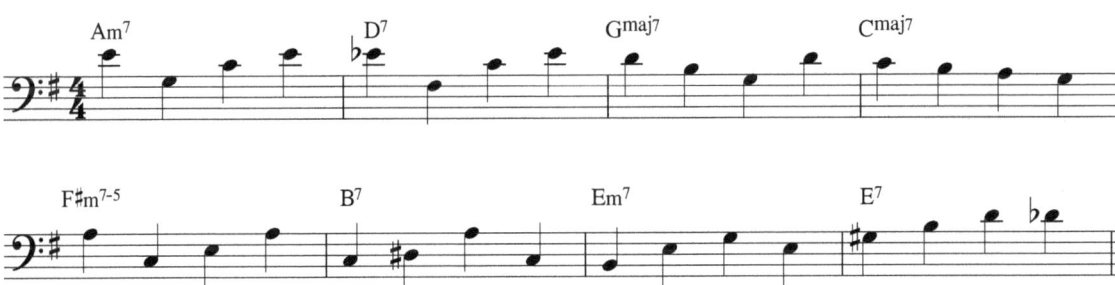

Example 17

Here is the full collection of descending ii°-V-i patterns, beginning from the 5th of the ii° chord. This pattern can start from any pitch in the ii° chord, though your choice of patterns will be governed by range: starting on Eb in the melody voice (the 5th of Am7b5) allows for a comfortable descent through all the patterns without running out of fingerboard space. The descending patterns are labeled based on the melody voice (or top note) of the ii chord.

The difference between the predominant chord shapes, which is determined by the previous position, is whether the root or 7th is included. In examples where the root is not present in the predominant chord, the chord becomes an inversion of a C Minor chord (the iv chord in G Minor). Though each position presents more considerations than a ii-V-I in major, a ii°-V-i in minor can still be executed in almost every position with a strong resolution. The only chord tone that is not used is as a starting place is the seventh, which does not contain a strong, usable resolution.

From the 5th of the ii° chord:

In this position, the root is not present in the ii° chord. This allows you to either use shape A or B for the dominant chord. The tonic resolution also has two options, resolving the F# upwards to G or to the F (the seventh). Resolving to the tonic provides a more convincing resolution, though it may not be easily accessible in every position.

Example 18a

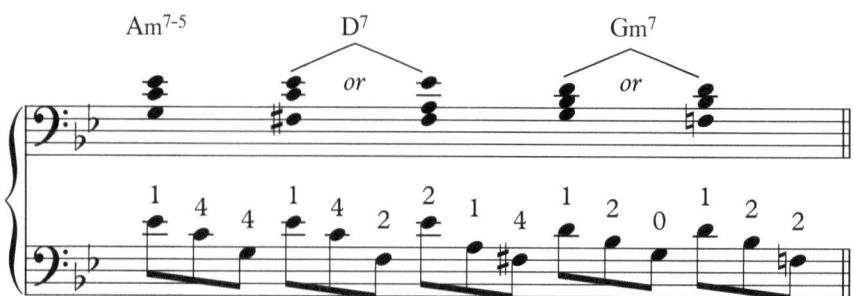

100

Example 18b

Variations on both the dominant and tonic chord are used here in a walking context.

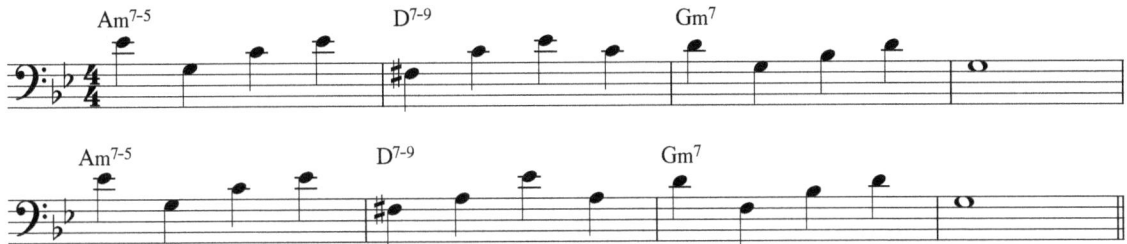

From the 3rd of the ii° chord:

In this position, there are two options for the predominant chord. Though there is another dominant chord option (Shape A), it is exactly the same as the second predominant option. The F# (as opposed to an A) provides stronger voice leading to the tonic, and is a far better choice in this position.

Example 19a

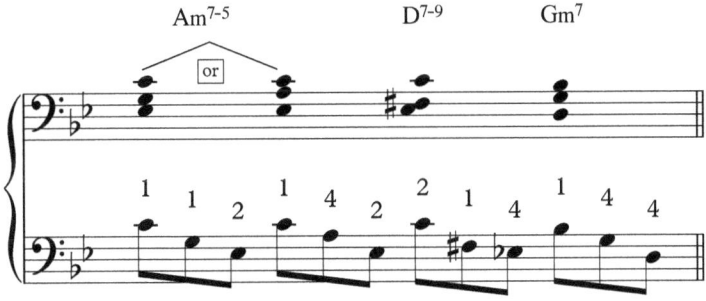

Example 19b

This walking example demonstrates the variation in the predominant choice.

From the root of the ii° chord:

This position offers the fewest number of variables. As the predominant chord is exactly the same as the dominant shape B, there is only one option for the dominant chord.

Example 20a

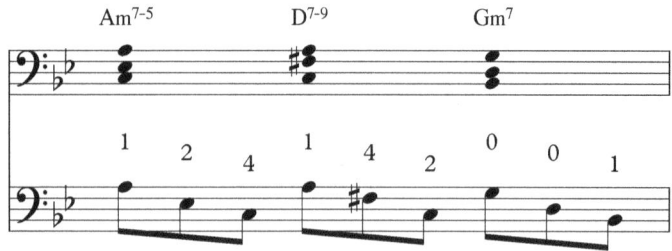

Example 20b

Here is the progression realized in a walking context.

Exercises

Exercise 6 - Using descending ii°-V-i's in in walking situations

Here are the same patterns realized in a walking context, progressing through the collection of ii°-V-i chords from Example 16. Inserting these patterns into walking bass lines is quite easy—wherever there is a minor ii°-V-i, practice incorporating these ideas into your lines.

Exercise 7 - Incorporating the VI chord between positions

Now that we're familiar with using the VI chord to move to ii in major, we can apply it to minor keys with equal impact. Practice the following at a medium tempo to gain familiarity. The dominant chords will either utilize Shape A or B, except for the last measure.

Exercise 8 - Moving around the bass

This progression uses a dominant chord to pivot to an unrelated key. Look for reuse of the same dominant VI chords in different keys. Though measures 6 and 16 contain they same notes, they can both be used to tonicize different tonic sounds.

Exercises

Sample 1 - "Autumn Leaves"

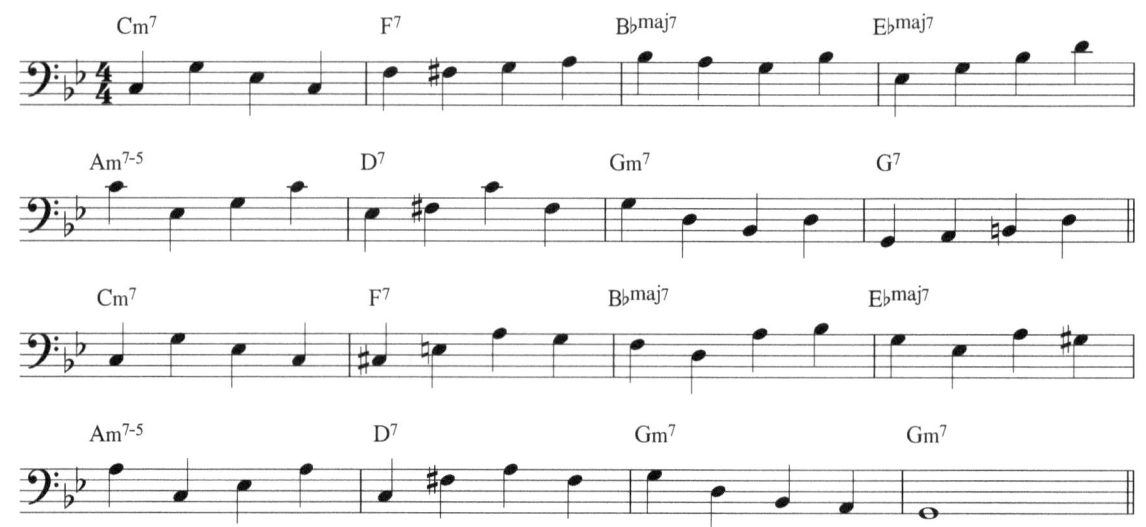

Sample 2 - "Woody 'n' You"

Ascending chord sequences - Major:

It is considerably more difficult to resolve V7 chords upwards than downwards, particularly with the b9 tension. As the b9 and 7th tends to resolve downwards (Example 21), resolving these tensions upwards—against their natural tendencies—can sound wrong.

Example 21

It is critically important to resolve these tensions, otherwise the supportive nature of the bass lines suffers. In this example, the third pattern is the only one to properly resolve all tensions. Patterns from the 7th are not included as the resolution is identical to the patterns from the root—a stronger harmonic choice.

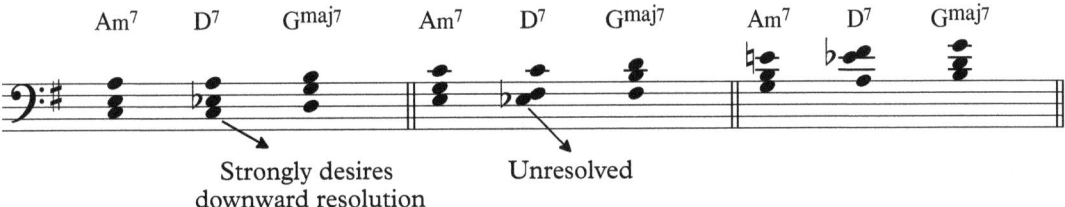

Ascending resolutions will require substituting the dominant chord with other sounds. Though it is possible to resolve V7b9 chords downwards, this section will focus on resolving tension upwards using diminished chords as a substitute for the dominant sound.

The diminished shapes you see will be similar to the diminished shapes in earlier chapters. Though fingered the same, they function differently.

Example 22

In place of D7, we will use a A#° (fully diminished) chord when appropriate. As the diminished chord is symmetrical, it technically has four roots, and all of the diminished inversions provide strong voice leading to G Major.

Example 23

Here is the full collection of ascending ii-V-I patterns, beginning from the Root of the ii chord. This pattern can start from any pitch in the ii chord, though your choice of patterns will be governed by range: starting on A in the melody voice (the Root of Am7) allows for a comfortable ascent through all the patterns. The ascending patterns are labeled based on the melody voice (or top note) of the ii chord. A diminished chord is used in place of the dominant sounds where appropriate.

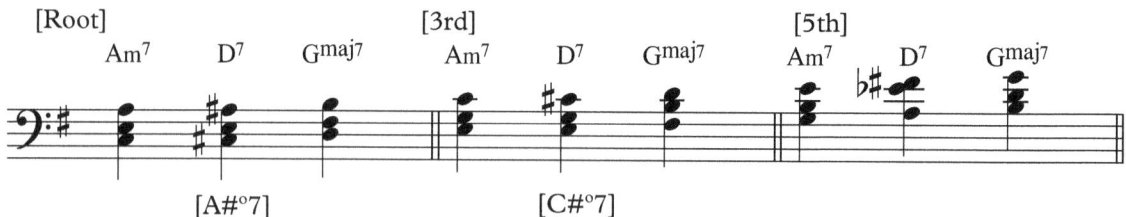

Though there is a clash when comparing D7 to A# diminished, the A# diminished does function as a dominant sound. Dominant harmony emphasizes the move to tonic through the thirds and sevenths; the most important chord tones for defining harmony. The seventh of the dominant chord resolves down to the third of the tonic chord, and the third of the dominant chord becomes the seventh of the tonic. These half step exchanges are what completes the resolution to the tonic.

Diminished chords also emphasize the chord tones in tonic by half step, but these notes resolve up to the tonic instead of down. There may be a clash if the pianist or guitarist voices a dominant sound while you outline a diminished chord, but the integrity of the line is still there. Most importantly, both chords resolve to the tonic.

You can think of this concept in two additional ways:
- F#7b9 tonicizing B minor (which functions the same as G Major in this instance)
- F#7 tonicizing G Major. This half step upwards movement to the tonic functions as a dominant sound.

From the Root of the ii chord:

In this example, an A#° chord is used in place of D7 to emphasize the move to an inversion G Major. Even though C is the lowest note in the ii chord, A still functions as the root.

Example 24a

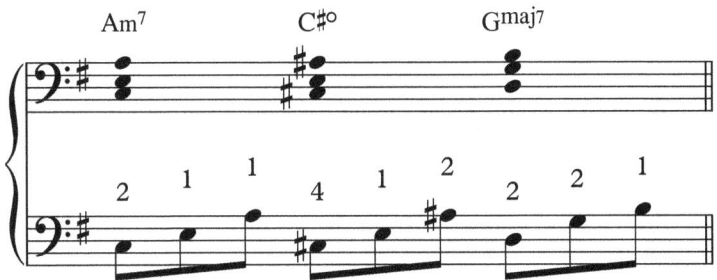

SD 1-2-3 in the tonic

Example 24b

Applying Example 23a to a walking bass looks like this:

Example 24c

In this example, A# diminished voice leads to G/D. This works by emphasizing the move to the 5th and 3rd of G—two stable and strong chord tones. Notice the similarity to the 6th motion from Chapter 2.

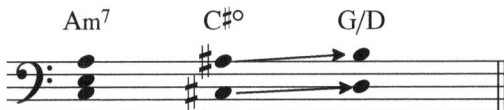

From the Root of the ii chord:

In this example, an A#° chord is used in place of D7 to emphasize the move to an inversion G Major. Even though C is the lowest note in the ii chord, A still functions as the root.

Example 25a

SD 4-#4-5 in the tonic

Example 25b

Here is Example 25a applied in a walking context:

From the 5th of the ii chord:

In this position the ascending diminished chord is not used as the 7b9 shape resolves effectively.

Example 26a

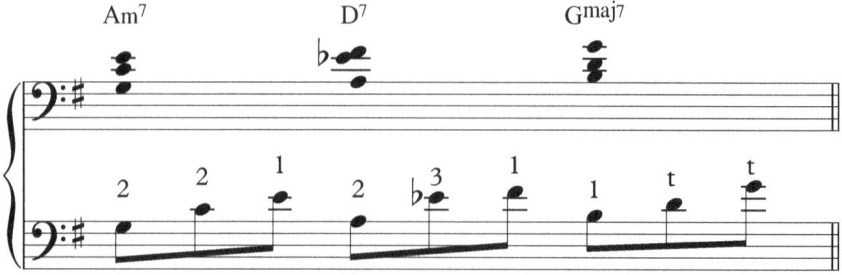

SD 6-7-8 in the tonic

Example 26b

Here is example 26a in a walking bass line:

Exercises

Exercise 9 - Using ascending ii-V-I's in in walking situations

Here are the same patterns realized in a walking context, progressing through the collection of ii-V-I chords from Example 23. Inserting these patterns into walking bass lines is quite easy—wherever there is a major ii-V-I, practice incorporating these ideas into your lines.

Exercise 10 - Connecting all the patterns using the VI chord

Similar to Exercise 2, in which the VI chord linked descending ii-V-I progressions, the VI chord (or appropriate diminished substitution) can be used to connect ascending ii-V-I patterns. Here are the ii-V-I examples in their full realization, using ascending diminished sounds instead of dominant. Take note how the outside of the shape—the 6ths—are still present like every other example.

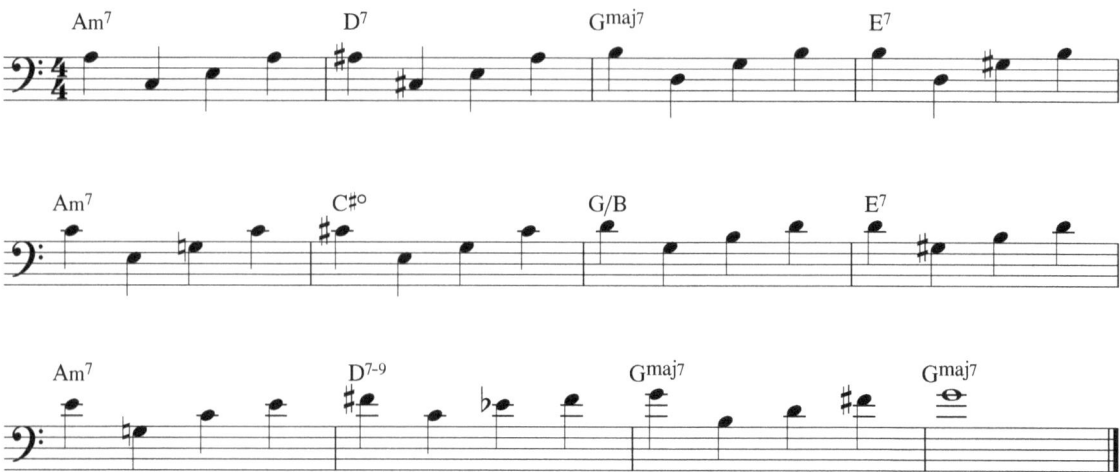

Sample bass lines

In these examples the ascending diminished chord is used (and noted) wherever possible.

Sample 3 - "Autumn Leaves"

Sample 4 - "In a Mellow Tone"

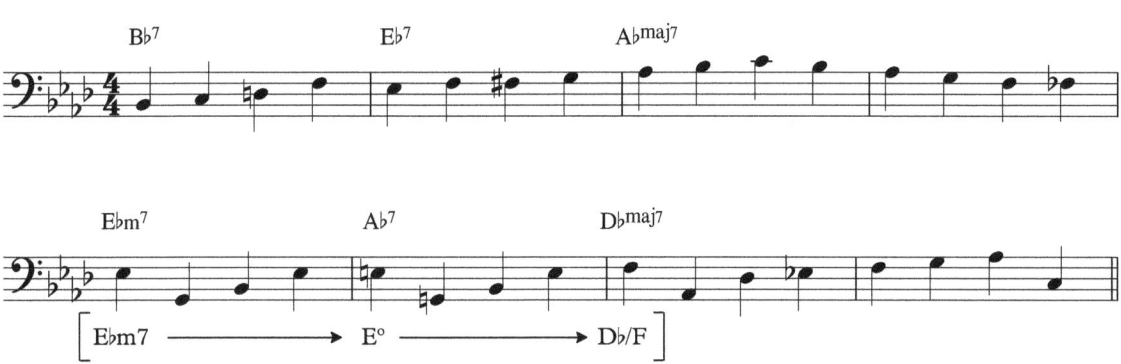

Traveling Melody Note:

Ascending ii°-V-i chord progressions is not practical in minor, as the presence of the b9 in dominant chords naturally resolves downwards. The only possibility for ascension is through traveling. Traveling melody notes works in any context and is not specific to ascending through minor ii°-V-i chord progressions.

As I mentioned when discussing ascending major sequences, individual chords do not have to resolve to their closest neighboring chords and can instead travel freely around the instrument while maintaining strong harmonic support of the melody and solo lines. The voice leading works such that you can move between positions and still create smooth melodic movement. This allows for more melodic bass lines and will strengthen your understanding of the fingerboard. The top note (melody voice) in each arpeggio will be the guiding note when creating your line; always relate your melody note to the overall key you are in.

Tip: When traveling it's easiest to divide the ii-V-I into two sections: the ii chord, and the V-I resolution. This allows you to conceptualize the progression into two parts instead of three.

You can travel wide distances around the fingerboard and still complete a melodic ii-V-I. This, of course, depends on the the context at the time—if there is a melody being played, etc—and what range you want your line to exist in. The following are a few of many possibilities to travel. Again, consider the highest note when making your choices.

Example 27a - Ascending travel in minor

You cannot ascend entirely through minor iiº-V progressions without traveling. Example 27a places distance between the iiº and V7 chords before resolving to the closest available tonic chord. Look for the differences between shape A & B, particularly between the iiº and V7 chords.

Example 27b - Ascending and descending in minor

Example 27b travels in both ascending and descending directions.

Example 28 - "What Is This Thing Called Love"

"What Is This Thing Called Love" is useful tune to practice traveling minor ii-V-I's. Even though the second progression resolves to major, the first two chords still function as if they were in minor.

Example 29 - Traveling in major

Example 29 travels in both directions in the major key. The first line of Example 29 conceptualizes melody note movement of a ii-V-I as scale degree 4-2-3. Scale degrees 2-3 represents the dominant to tonic relationship.

Example 30a - "Perdido"

The first 16 bars of "Perdido" by Duke Ellington present a great opportunity to practice traveling in major, using ascending diminished chords and the VI chord.

Tip: Identify the various V-I relationships within the chord sequence. For example:

Example 30b

See if you can identify where the melody note travels (by scale degree), and, the groupings of V-I relationships.

Example 30c—"Cherokee" (Bridge)

See if you can identify where the melody note travels (by scale degree), and, the groupings of V-I relationships.

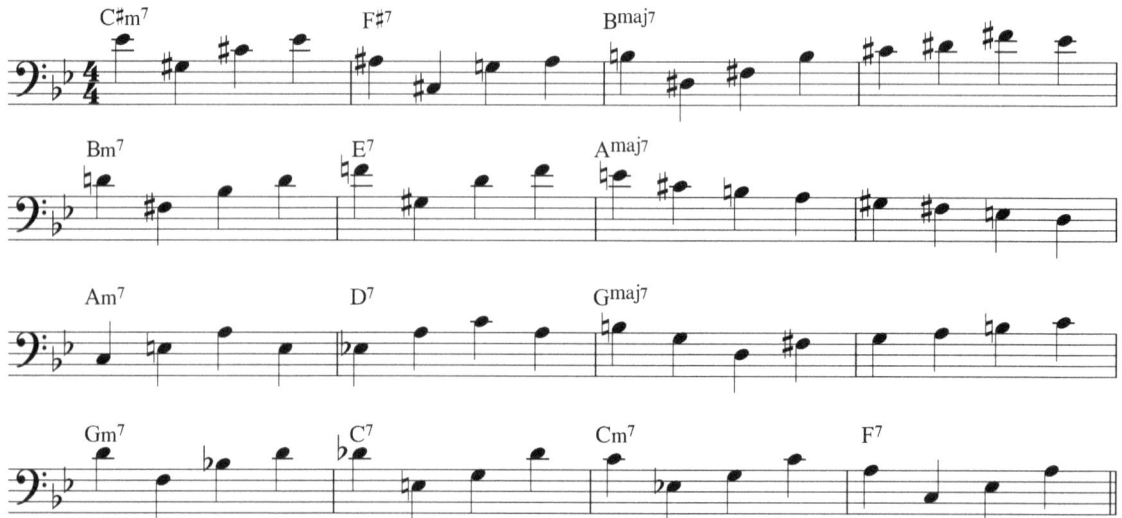

Reiterating the importance of the melody:

With all this talk of being melodic, it's important to reiterate the necessity of knowing the melody. There are two basic situations where one walks bass lines—behind a melody or behind a soloist. In both cases it pays to know the melody, but in the former it is essential to know the melody. You must know the melody in order to support it. This is particularly true when generating bass lines that are only comprised of chord tones. With many melodies to American Songbook comprised of 3rds, 7ths and other chord tones, one can easily nullify counterpoint with their bass line. Behind a soloist you have more flexibility with your note choices, but you only have two chances to support the melody.

Sample bass lines

Integrating all concepts:

Here are final samples that incorporate all of the techniques taught in this chapter. Look for ascending ii-V-I patterns using diminished chords, descending stationary patterns, and traveling melody notes. See how many techniques you can identify.

Sample 5 - "Perdido"
Sample 6 - "Just Friends"
Sample 7 - "Autumn Leaves"

Sample 5 - "Perdido"

Chorus 1

Chorus 2

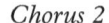

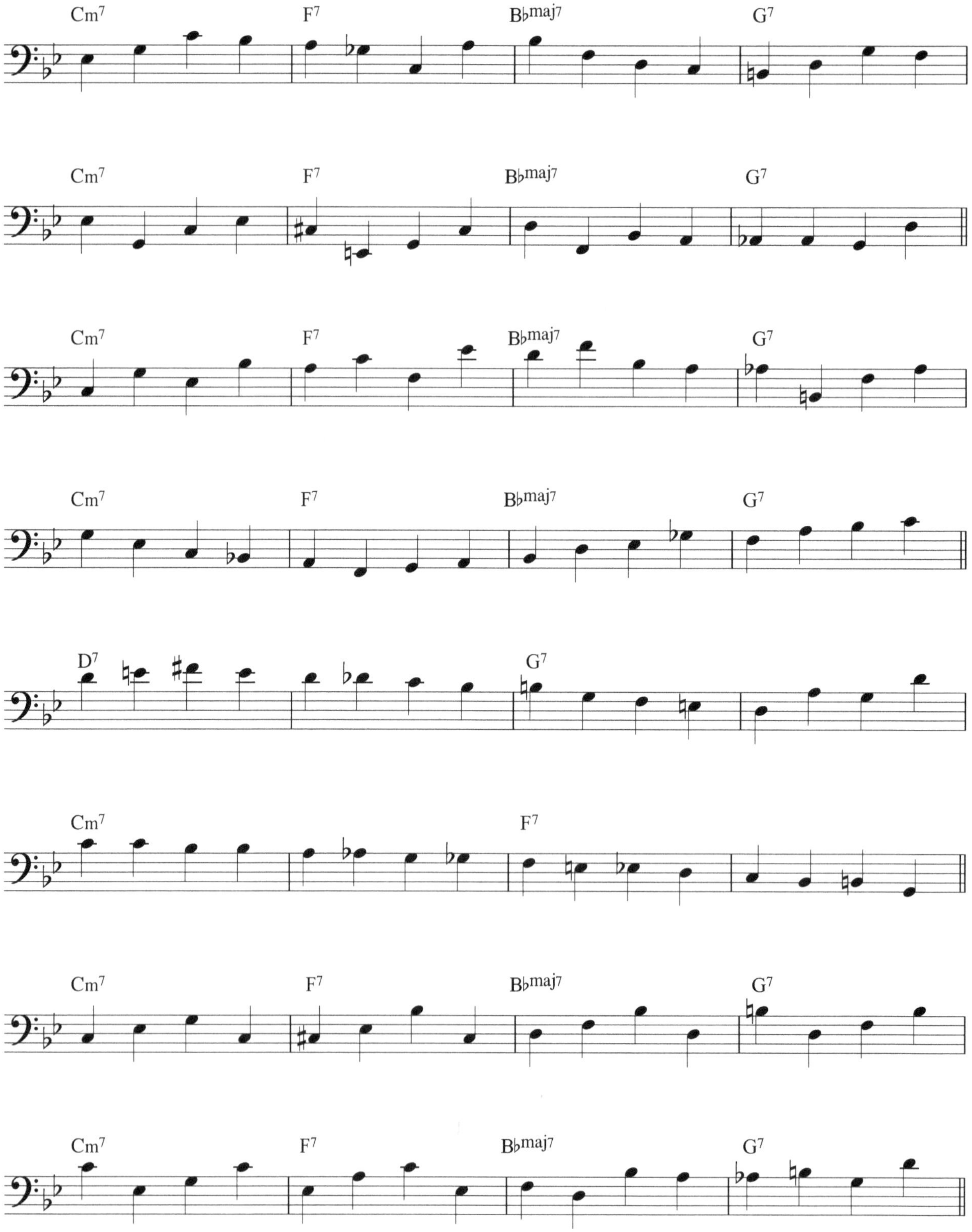
Cm7 F7 B♭maj7 G7
Cm7 F7 B♭maj7 G7
Cm7 F7 B♭maj7 G7
Cm7 F7 B♭maj7 G7
D7 G7
Cm7 F7
Cm7 F7 B♭maj7 G7
Cm7 F7 B♭maj7 G7

Chorus 3

Sample 6 - "Just Friends"

Chorus 1

Chorus 2

125

Chorus 3

Sample 7 - "Autumn Leaves"

Chorus 1

Chorus 2

Chorus 3

129

Chapter 4

Reduction Harmony

Chapter 4

This chapter will explore a technique called **Reduction Harmony**, which simplifies the amount of information in a two-measure ii-V-I:

Example 1a

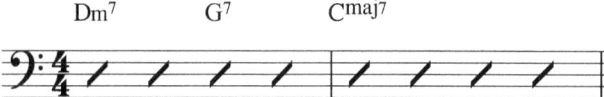

This technique is used by treating a ii-V-I as a V-I, applying the notes of a dominant chord over the predominant chord. The predominant is not entirely ignored, but rather utilizes the common notes between the dominant and predominant in such a way that it sounds like you are addressing both chords (though the structure is entirely dominant). This essentially makes the dominant four beats long instead of two, and will be the most common approach discussed in the chapter. With Reduction Harmony, we will be addressing the macro harmony instead of micro harmony. This technique is particularly useful to add tension, emphasis, or affect the harmonic rhythm. Use of this technique in conjunction with other common walking bass vocabulary will yield more musical and meaningful bass lines.

Reduction Harmony slows the harmonic rhythm, creating a more grounded feel in the music. Too much harmonic movement can feel frenetic and limit options for walking. When reducing harmony the music still maintains its forward motion, but feels less busy as the perceived harmony is lessened. This macro harmonic approach also fosters the development of longer phrases, which in turn promote more melodic bass lines. A micro harmony approach can produce walking and solo bass lines that lack connectivity. Soloists will often contrast harmonically dense lines with lines just addressing dominant and tonic; these reduced lines create a sense of connectedness in the music and provide a release of tension.

Throughout the examples in this chapter, the dominant chord functions the same in both major and minor ii-V-I progressions, even with the V7b9. Your ears will ultimately govern your harmonic choices, though I will provide considerations for using diatonic vs. dominant sounds with a b9. Primary tunes will include Confirmation, Stablemates, Have You Met Miss Jones, You Go To My Head, and Giant Steps. These tunes cover a variety of harmonic progressions from the American Songbook, bebop, and hard bop tradition. Before applying Reduction Harmony, it is important to understand why the predominant can be treated flexibly.

The theory behind Reduction Harmony:

In the hierarchy of Western harmony, the dominant chord follows only the tonic chord in terms of strength and stability. The dominant sound is what gives tonic its context; it is what makes tonic feel like "home." Tonic and dominant sounds are at the core Western harmony: from Bach's Well-Tempered Clavier and Cello Suites, to John Coltrane's "Giant Steps," and beyond. The ii-V-I progression is most often associated with jazz repertoire, even though progressions with a predominant chord (ii or IV) have been around for centuries in a variety of genres. Jazz musicians particularly favor the ii chord as it reinforces the dominant's move to the tonic chord, providing the soloist more harmony to incorporate into their improvisations. The addition of the ii chord also allows for more harmonic substitutions, which gives soloists more colors to choose from.

In the hierarchy of Western harmony, the dominant chord follows only the tonic chord in terms of strength and stability. The dominant sound is what gives tonic its context; it is what makes tonic feel like "home." Tonic and dominant sounds are at the core Western harmony: from Bach's Well-Tempered Clavier and Cello Suites, to John Coltrane's "Giant Steps," and beyond. The ii-V-I progression is most often associated with jazz repertoire, even though progressions with a predominant chord (ii or IV) have been around for centuries in a variety of genres. Jazz musicians particularly favor the ii chord as it reinforces the dominant's move to the tonic chord, providing the soloist more harmony to incorporate into their improvisations. The addition of the ii chord also allows for more harmonic substitutions, which gives soloists more colors to choose from.

The two basic ways of addressing a ii-V-I:

It's helpful to understand the two basic approaches to outlining a ii-V-I progression in walking bass: Vertical and Linear. When addressing ii-V-I progressions of two beats each, especially multiple ii-V-I's in succession, there are limited options to outline the harmony.

Vertical means articulating harmony in a single position with minimal shifting. The result is an arpeggiated type bass line. With the vertical approach, it is easy to identify the roots of the chord progression based on the articulated harmonies. Limited to two beats per chord, this approach requires bassists to articulate the shell of each chord change, resulting in a line where the root is emphasized by diatonic or chromatic notes. The root is the most dense note a bassist can play, because it adds the most harmonic weight to a chord.

Root to fifth:

Example 1b

In this example, the ii chord is outlined by a leap from the root to the fifth.

Passing tone to root:

Example 1c

In this example, the root of the ii chord is played on the downbeat, then the root of the V chord is approached chromatically.

These vertical examples draw attention to the root by placing them on beats 1 & 3, the strong beats. This is necessary at times, but overuse can create harmonically anemic bass lines due to a lack of inner harmony. Vertical bass lines, regardless of whether the root is approached diatonically or chromatically, generally have the same impact on the music.

Linear means addressing harmony in a scale like movement to build tension and emphasize important markers in the form. The result is a bass line with a longer trajectory. With the linear approach, it may be difficult to identify the chord progression based on the articulated harmonies. As with the vertical approach, you can approach linear bass lines diatonically or chromatically.

Example 2a

Example 2b

Both linear lines approach the target note (the tonic) similarly, stepwise motion from either above or below the chord.

Applying it to walking:

Reduction Harmony uses the common notes between the dominant and predominant chords in such a way that it sounds like you are outlining both chords, though the four-note structure is entirely dominant. When walking a ii-V-I where the ii and V both are two beats long, a V7 chord contains chord tones that will strongly outline the ii chord. This has to do with their shared notes, referring to notes that are common to both the ii and V7 chord.

> **The ii and V7 contains two shared notes: chord degrees 1 and 3 of the ii chord.**

Example 3a

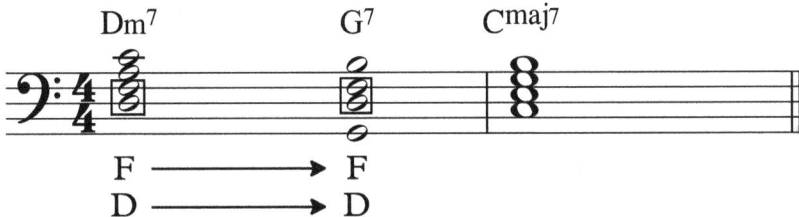

Example 3b

Lining up the chord changes also helps to visually identify the shared information.

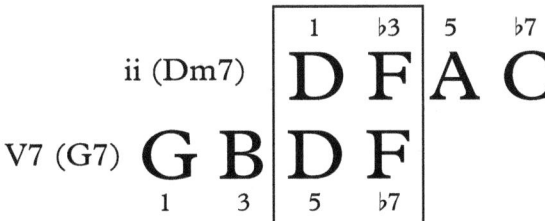

By arpeggiating V7 in such a way that it first expresses the two shared notes on beats one and two, you essentially reduce the harmony to dominant-tonic. Theoretically it looks as if you are articulating the ii chord purposefully, but the ear recognizes the entire shape as dominant. Try playing this on the bass; notice the contrast between diatonic neighbor tones and wide intervals.

Example 4a

Here are other ways to organize the shared notes in such a way that the ii chord is still outlined while only shaping the dominant chord. Any combination of octave displacements can be used. An index of reductions in all 12 major keys is provided in Exercise 1.

**The V7 shape begins on scale degrees 2 or 4 of the tonic key.
Looking for these notes this will help you incorporate the patterns quicker.**

Example 4b

Adjusting the order of notes:

As you learn to create these lines, keep in mind Key, Range, and Starting Pitch. These all determine when and how you incorporate these ideas.

You can begin your phrase on either of the shared notes, however certain keys will move the voice leading to the top or bottom of your instrument, reducing your options for building long moving lines through the instrument. When creating these lines, I find it easiest to conceptualize the triadic shapes from the top, letting the top note be the melodic guide. Typically I use a High, Low, Mid note approach, and then a High, Mid, Low. Sometimes I articulate the middle voice first—it all depends on the context.

Reordering pitches gives full control over subtle harmonic details, like delaying a b9, and make it easier to visualize the voice leading.

Example 5

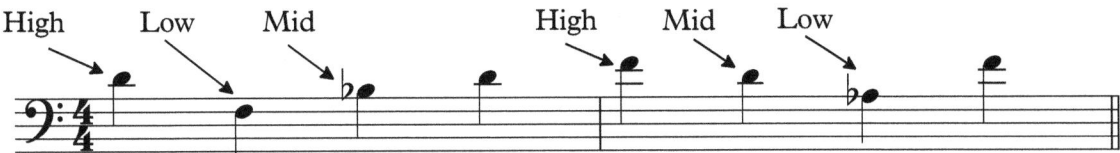

As you move through this chapter and write your own bass lines, experiment with the order of the shared notes and the rest of the triad. As you learn to integrate this idea into your bass lines, you'll soon form a preference that reflects your musical taste.

Walking contexts

One significant advantage to Reduction Harmony, besides increasing melodicism, is that it reduces the number of changes you have to manage, making it much easier to walk uptempo tunes. Let's look at "Giant Steps," a tune with many ii-V-I's that move around quickly.

Example 6a - "Giant Steps"

A common method of walking uptempo tunes is to outline the root movement using half steps or linear scale approaches. If you look at beats 1 & 3 of the ii-V's, the line is little more than root motion. This line is functional, but provides little melodic interest.

By essentially skipping each predominant chord, outlining only the V-I makes it easier to navigate the key centers by slowing harmonic rhythm, creating more melodic bass lines, and easing the amount of movement around the bass. Here are the isolated key V-I movements.

Example 6b - "Giant Steps"

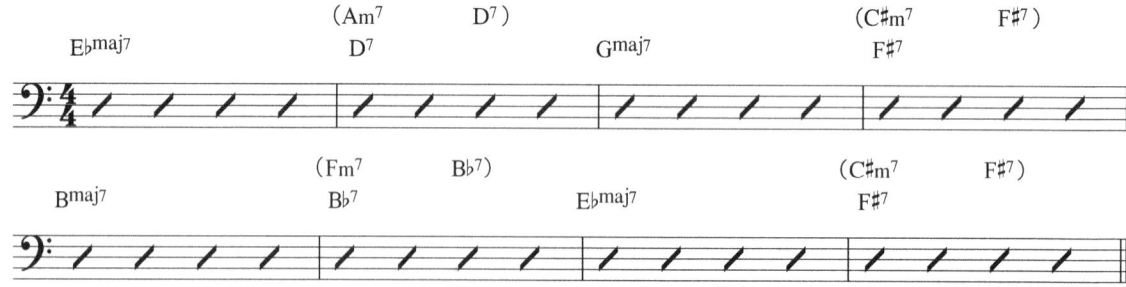

Example 6c - "Giant Steps"

Here is a demonstration just using V-I in the walking instead of the complete ii-V-I.

Example 6d - "Have You Met Miss Jones"

Here is a sample 8-bar bass line only using the V-I shapes over "Have You Met Miss Jones." Notice how the first two notes of the dominant shape also belong to the ii chord.

Adding tension with the V7b9:

The b9 adds harmonic color and tension without losing functionality, and resolves to the tonic chord.

Example 7a

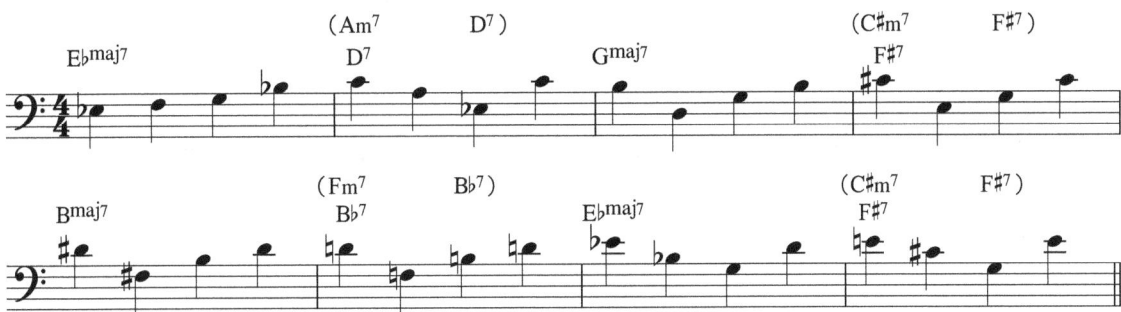

Example 7b

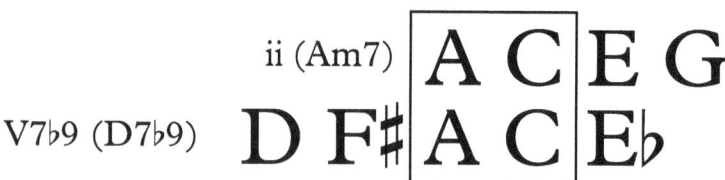

Example 7c

When the shared notes are articulated on beats one and two, the b9 of the dominant chord comes on the third beat of the measure—where the chord changes from predominant to a dominant sound. Though we "ignore" the predominant, the V7b9 shapes work because it expresses both harmonies at once without conflict.

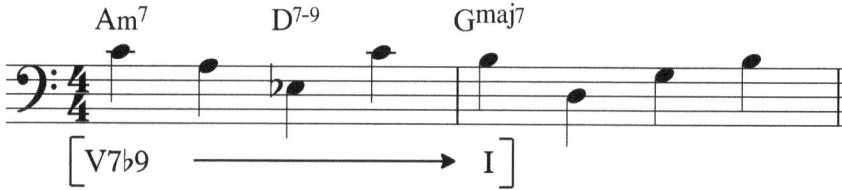

Example 7d

Disregarding the shared notes and freely using the b9 fundamentally changes the quality of the ii chord. A quality change in the predominant chord is not a substitution other musicians would listen actively for, and thus would result in a conflict. Here is an example of what not to do:

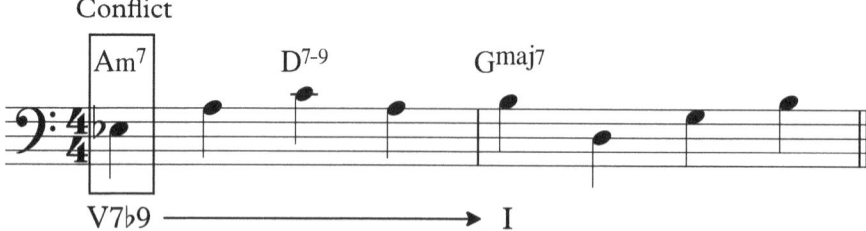

In short, you can interchange the V7b9 and V7 chords freely—so long as the quality of the ii chord is not impacted.

Exercises

Exercise 1 covers all the basic reductions and resolutions of ii-V7-I to V7-I in 12 keys; it does not account for octave displacement. Both diatonic and b9 dominant chords are represented, and marked according to what scale degree of the tonic they begin on. Practice this exercise to become familiar with the different shapes possible when using Reduction Harmony.

Exercise 2 provides opportunities to practice walking bass lines over ii-V-I progressions in all keys.

Exercise 1

142

Exercise 2

Bass Line Excerpts

Here are samples of the Reduction Harmony technique using both V7 and V7b9 in Major.

Excerpt 1 - "Stablemates"

Excerpt 2 - "You're My Everything"

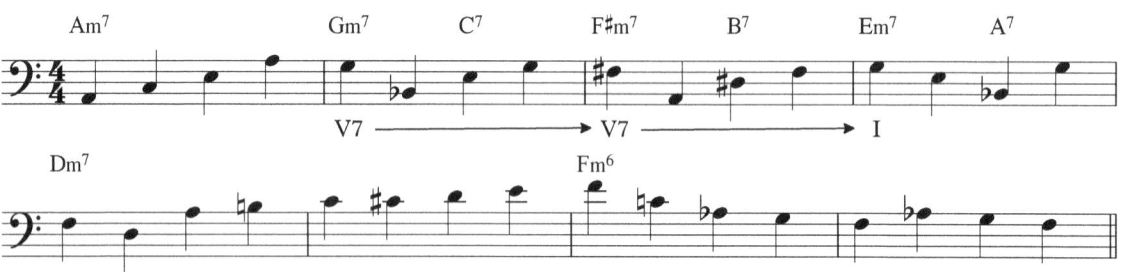

Excerpt 3 - "You Go To My Head"

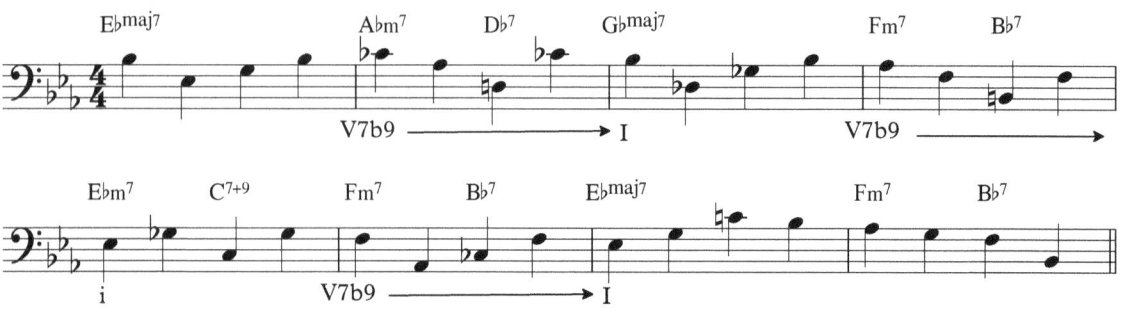

Reduction Harmony in Minor keys:

In jazz standards, you'll see ii-V-I progressions in both major and minor keys. The process of reducing the harmony in a minor ii-V-I of two beats per chord is the same as major. Aside from the change in the ii chord—min7 to diminished—the treatment of the progression is unchanged.

Example 8a

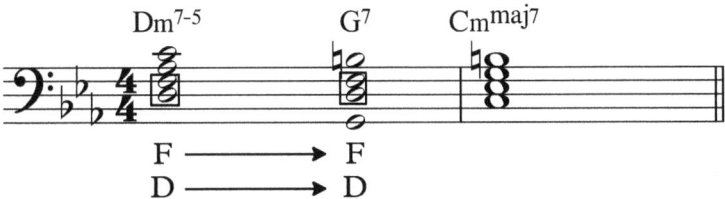

**The ii° and V7 contains the same shared notes:
chord degrees 1 and 3 of the ii chord.**

Example 8b

Lining up the chord changes also helps to visually identify the shared information.

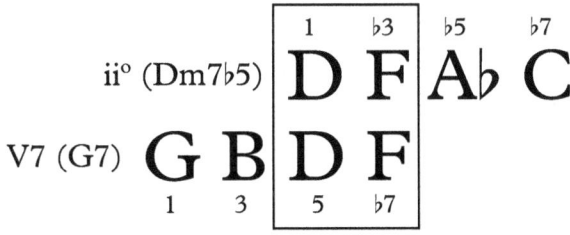

Similarities between ii° and V7b9:

When adding a b9 to a dominant chord, the core structure of the chord becomes diminished. In major examples, using a b9 would create a clash in the ii chord by changing the quality of the chord—unless the b9 was articulated on beat three. There is no clash in the minor key.

Between the ii° and V7b9, there are now three notes held in common: 1, b3, and b5 of the ii chord.

Example 8c

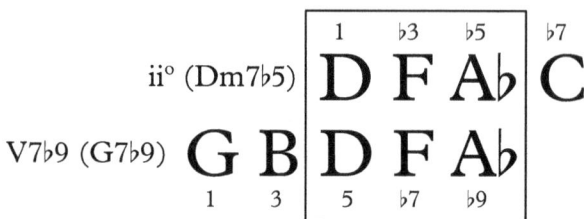

In jazz standards, you'll see ii-V-I progressions in both major and minor keys. The process of reducing the harmony in a minor ii-V-I of two beats per chord is the same as major. Aside from the change in the ii chord—min7 to diminished—the treatment of the progression is unchanged.

These shapes can start on scale degrees b6, 4 and 2 of the tonic. It is easiest to think in the tonic key.

Example 9

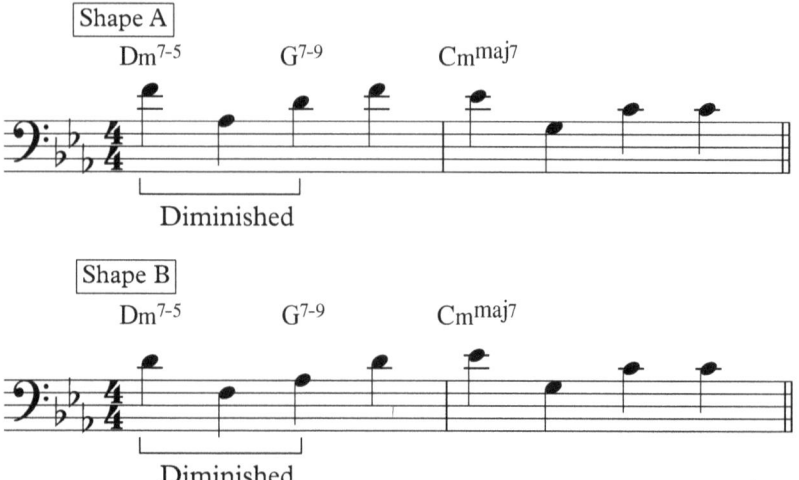

Similarities between diminished chords and dominant Shapes A and B:

In Chapter 1, there were many examples using Shape A or Shape B to represent varying dominant functions. Hopefully you are beginning to recognize dominant Shapes A and B with some ease.

In the previous example, "A" and "B" correlate to the dominant shape they represent. Dominant shapes "A" and "B" are diminished shapes. The two shapes are flexible in nature and can be used to represent harmony in major and minor, in both diatonic and altered forms. This volume is not the place to explore the deep relationship between these shapes and upper extensions over altered dominant sounds, but the curious practicer will surely find a way to connect the two ideas.

Minor ii°-V-i in context:

Thus far, all examples have used the shared notes from the diminished triad to represent predominant and dominant harmonies. When adding the 3rd of the dominant chord—a note that is not shared—possibilities arise that are similar to using the 7b9 in major. Example 11 demonstrates using shared notes and the 3rd of the dominant.

The second measure of a Parker Blues—Charlie Parker's reharmonization of the 12 bar blues—provides an opportunity to outline both the ii° and V chord with V7b9 (using Shape A). "Parker Blues" changes and "Confirmation", both by Charlie Parker, are similar in their harmonic progressions. The notes in the shape are reordered to place the third of the dominant on beat 3.

Example 10

The tonic in this example is D Minor. Shape A is used starting on b6 of the tonic.

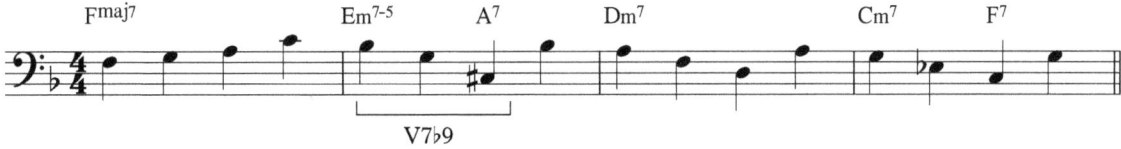

The next two examples are variations on Shapes A and B.

Example 11a

In this example, Shape B starts on the root of Am7b5—SD 2 of the tonic (G Minor). It is a simple diminished triad, but in the context of the ii°-V-i it outlines both the ii° and V by emphasizing the b9 of the dominant: A-C-Eb. If Shape B were used starting on the third of Am7b5 (scale degree 4 of the tonic), it would emphasize the third of the dominant: C-Eb-F#.

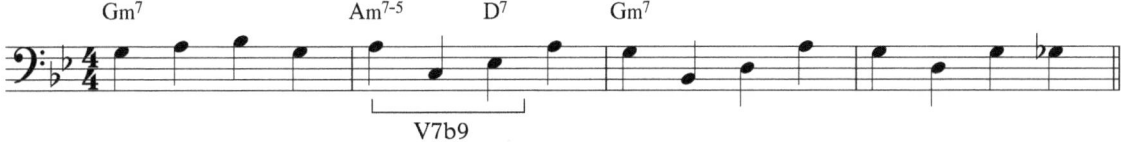

151

Example 11b

Shape A still represents a diminished chord, but more directly represents the dominant function with the presence of F#, the 3rd. If shape A was used beginning on the 3rd of Am7b5 (scale degree 2 of tonic), it would outline C-Eb-A—a more literal diminished shape.

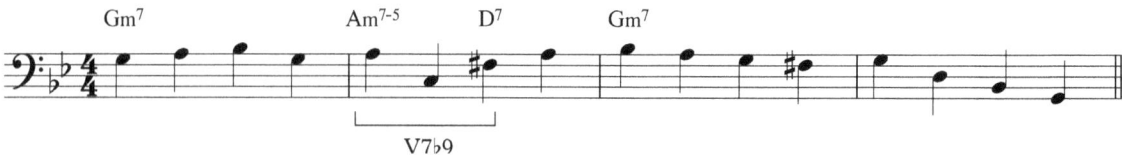

Both shapes will represent predominant and dominant function from every chord tone in the ii chord, except for the 7th. It's not as important to memorize the exact positions, but knowing that almost anything is a possibility helps when reducing harmony.

Exercises

Exercise 3 provides some (but not all) of the options for applying shared notes to a ii°-V-i. There are at least eight options per key, depending on what shape and starting pitch you use. This should serve as a reference guide as you continue to explore the myriad possibilities. Measures with two notes illustrate multiple options for resolving your lines. Practice this exercise to become familiar with the different shapes possible when using Reduction Harmony.

Exercise 4 provides a few examples of how you might apply the diminished shape to your bass line vocabulary in all 12 keys. Look for instances of both Shapes A and B.

Exercise 3

Exercise 4

Sample bass lines

These sample tunes use the Reduction Harmony technique in major and minor keys. Look for the instances of V-I, and try to identify from which starting pitch (both in relation to the ii chord and tonic) the technique is used.

Sample 1 - "Parker Blues"
Sample 2 - "Confirmation"
Sample 3 - "Giant Steps"
Sample 4 - "You Go To My Head"

Sample 1 - "Parker Blues"

Chorus 4

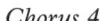

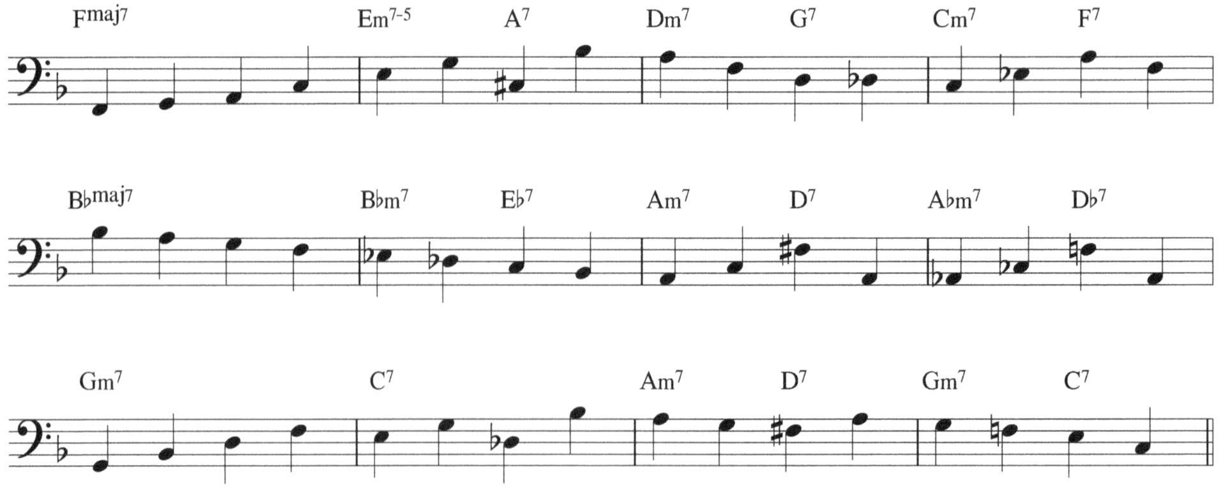

Chorus 5

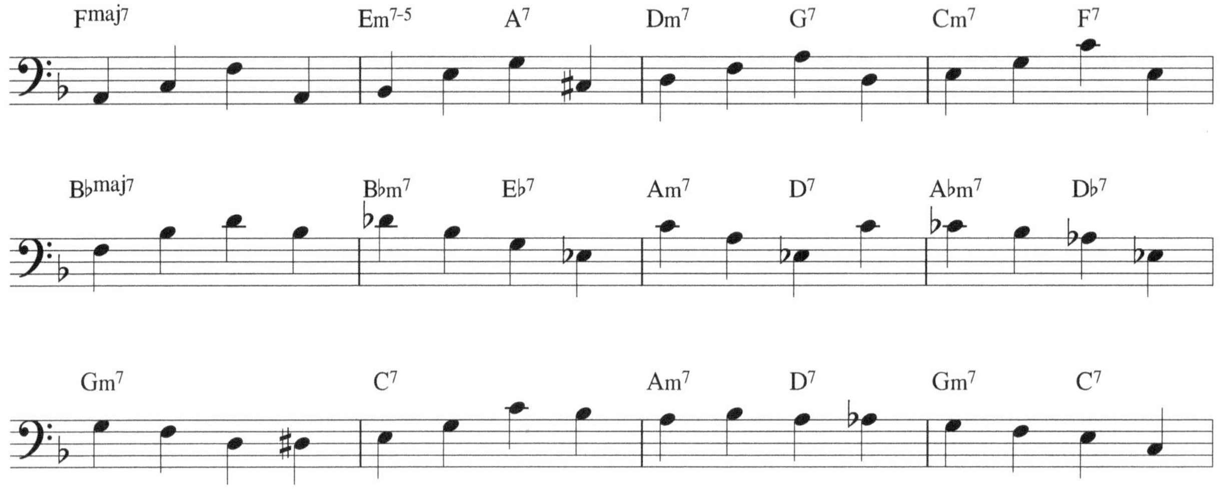

Chorus 6

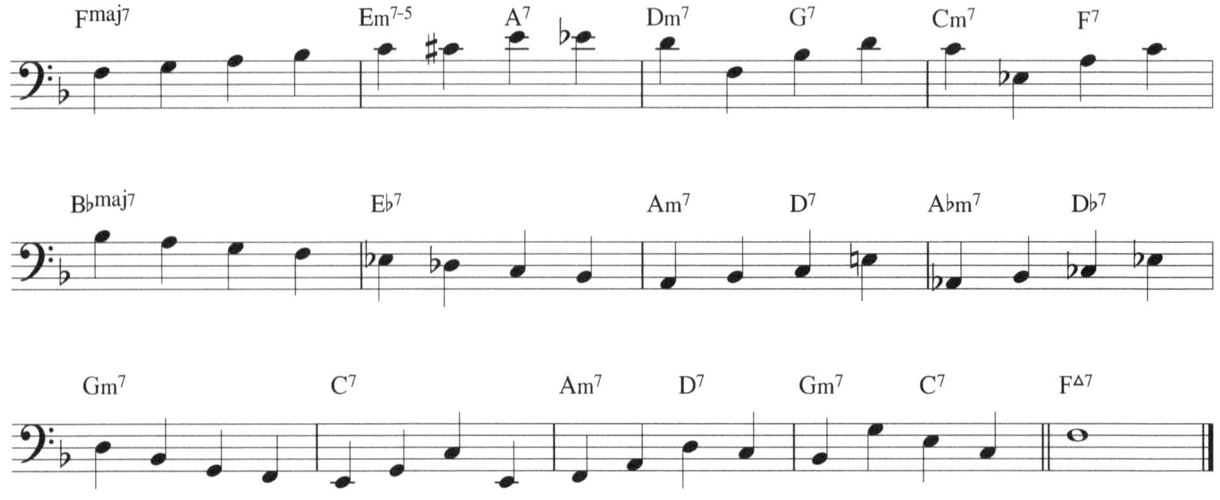

Sample 2 - "Confirmation"

Chorus 1

Chorus 2

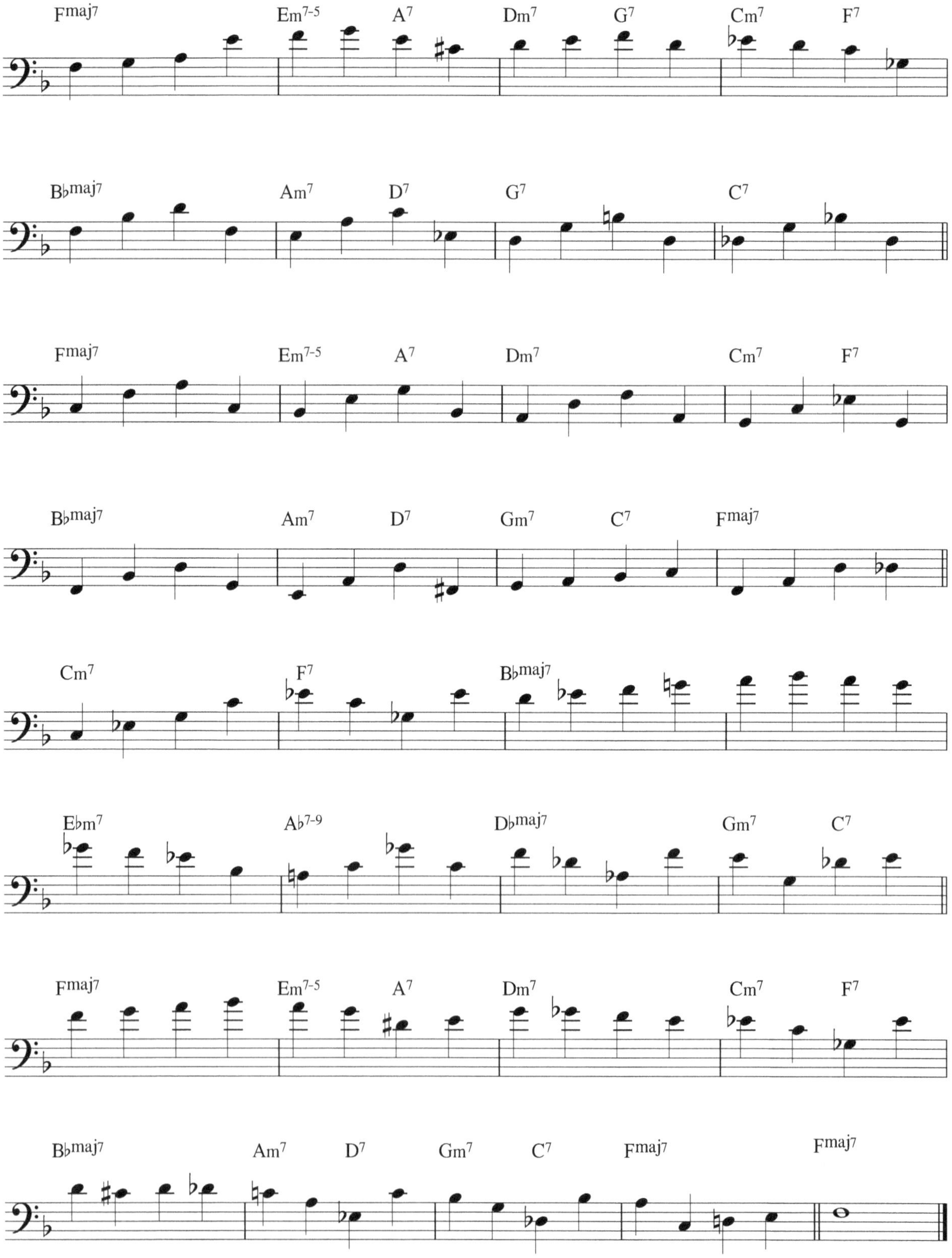
Fmaj7 Em7-5 A7 Dm7 G7 Cm7 F7
B♭maj7 Am7 D7 G7 C7
Fmaj7 Em7-5 A7 Dm7 Cm7 F7
B♭maj7 Am7 D7 Gm7 C7 Fmaj7
Cm7 F7 B♭maj7
E♭m7 A♭7-9 D♭maj7 Gm7 C7
Fmaj7 Em7-5 A7 Dm7 Cm7 F7
B♭maj7 Am7 D7 Gm7 C7 Fmaj7 Fmaj7

Sample 3 - "Giant Steps"

Sample 4 - "You Go To My Head"

Chorus 1

167

Chorus 2

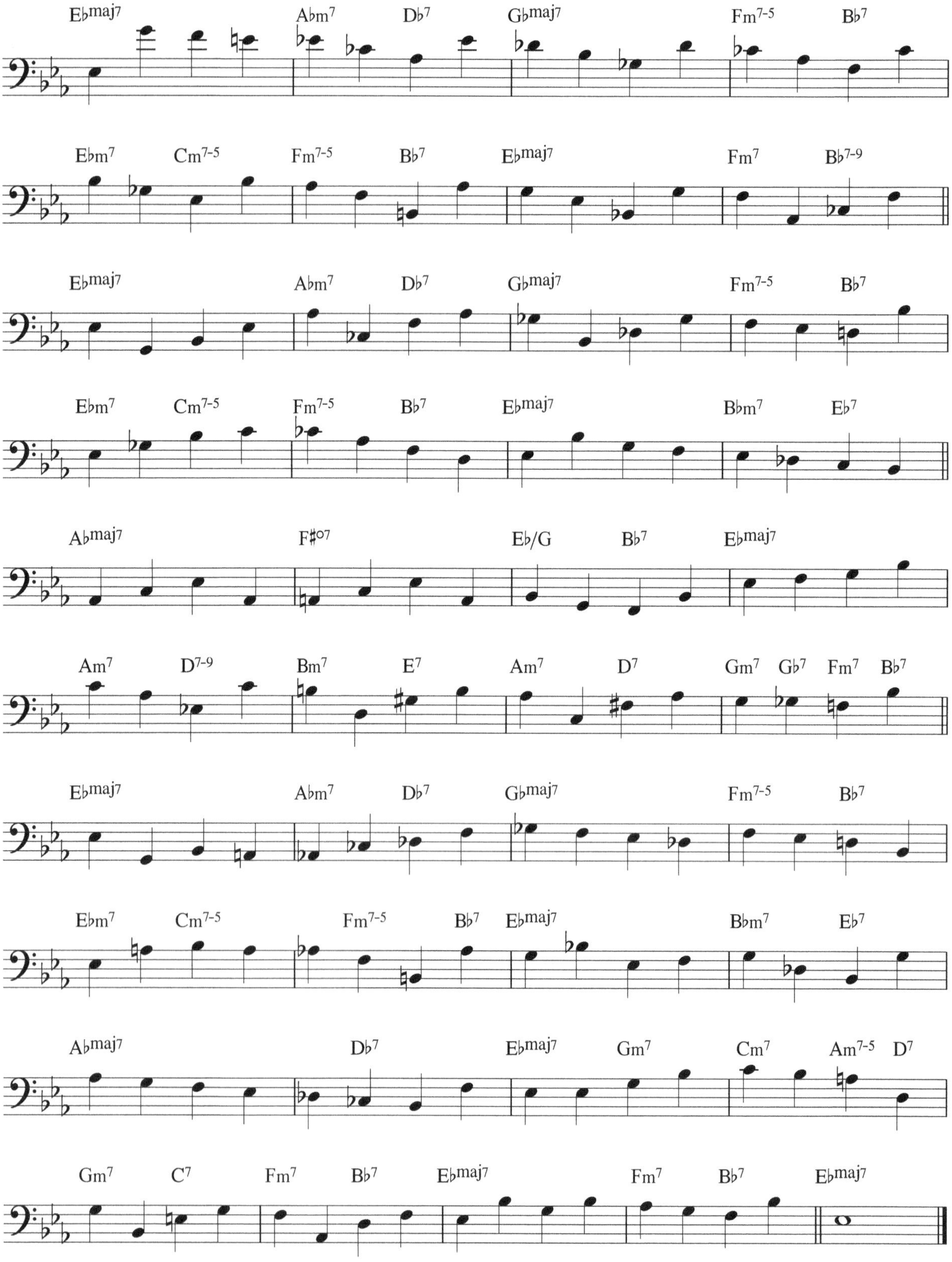
E♭maj7 A♭m7 D♭7 G♭maj7 Fm7-5 B♭7
E♭m7 Cm7-5 Fm7-5 B♭7 E♭maj7 Fm7 B♭7-9
E♭maj7 A♭m7 D♭7 G♭maj7 Fm7-5 B♭7
E♭m7 Cm7-5 Fm7-5 B♭7 E♭maj7 B♭m7 E♭7
A♭maj7 F♯o7 E♭/G B♭7 E♭maj7
Am7 D7-9 Bm7 E7 Am7 D7 Gm7 G♭7 Fm7 B♭7
E♭maj7 A♭m7 D♭7 G♭maj7 Fm7-5 B♭7
E♭m7 Cm7-5 Fm7-5 B♭7 E♭maj7 B♭m7 E♭7
A♭maj7 D♭7 E♭maj7 Gm7 Cm7 Am7-5 D7
Gm7 C7 Fm7 B♭7 E♭maj7 Fm7 B♭7 E♭maj7

Chapter 9 Reduction Harmony

Chapter 5

Reduction Harmony II—Rhythm Changes

Reduction Harmony over A sections

This book assumes the reader will have some familiarity with rhythm changes. For more information on rhythm changes, look at The Low Down, Vol. 1 and 2

"Rhythm changes" refers to the chord progression from George Gershwin's "I Got Rhythm," as important as the Blues in terms of "need-to-know" chord progressions. Rhythm changes can be a crux in bass player's walking line vocabulary. As with most quick-moving harmonic rhythms, it's easiest to outline the shell of the harmonic information, emphasizing the less harmonically rich note available. A common bass line looks like:

Example 1a

Even with many ways to outline the changes, I find bass players tend to address rhythm changes vertically. The Reduction Harmony technique can be used with extremely melodic results over rhythm changes. This will require chunking harmonic information into larger more accessible patterns, and identifying what is happening at the most fundamental harmonic levels.

We'll primarily focus on the A section, organizing it into three parts. Sections I and Section III are identical.

Example 1b

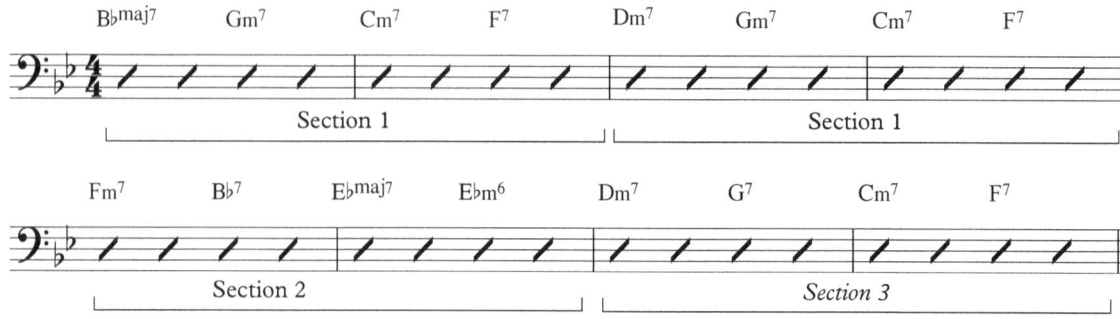

Section I: The I-vi-ii-V progression (Measures 1-4)
Section II: The move from I7-IV (Measures 5-6)
Section III: The iii-VI-ii-V progression (Measures 7-8)

How does it work?

Identifying shared notes in each measure facilitates reducing two harmonies to one function. This effectively slows the harmonic rhythm and creates a much more melodic bass line. The examples will begin with the most simple diatonic changes before introducing other substitutions common to rhythm changes.

The same process from before of reordering the notes will be applied here, typically following a High, Low, Mid structure. The shared notes will always fall on beats 1 & 2. Alterations and substitute chord changes will be addressed later in the chapter.

Example 2

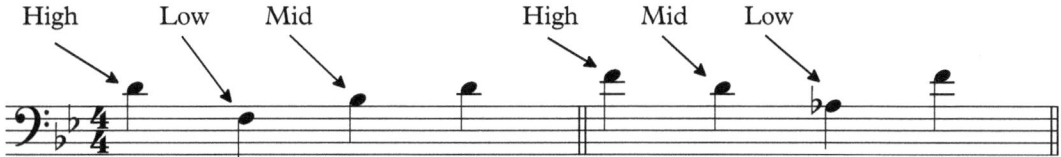

I, iii, and vi:

The I and iii chord hold three notes in common: Scale Degrees (SD) 3, 5, and 7 of the tonic. The I and vi hold three notes in common: SD 1, 3, 5 of tonic. The I chord will be used for all tonic chords now; later the iii chord will be introduced.

Example 3a

Example 3b

Here is a one measure sample utilizing these two chords with a value of two beats each. You can begin from either the root or the third of the tonic and represent the same sound.

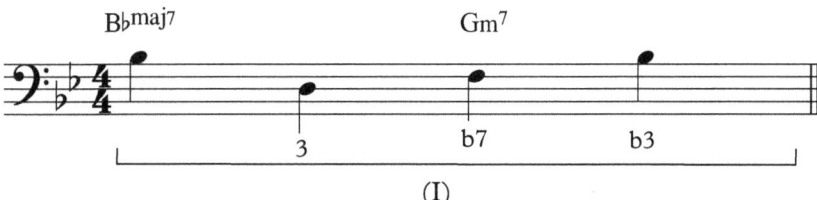

173

ii and V7:

This information was covered in Chapter 4 (Example 3b). To review, two notes are held in common between ii-V7: SD 2 and 4 of the tonic key.

Example 4a

Example 4b

Here is a one measure sample using these two chords with a value of two beats each.

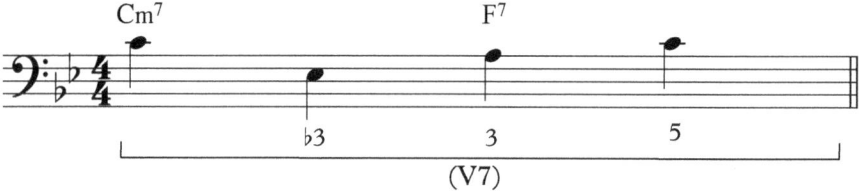

Starting from chord tones besides the root of the ii chord will introduce alterations, which we will discuss later.

Sections 1 and 3: I-vi-ii-V (or iii-vi-ii-V):

This concept will form the foundation for Reduction Harmony over rhythm changes:

> I – iii – vi = Tonic
> ii – V = Dominant

Example 5a

When reduced, a I-vi-ii-V (the first four bars of rhythm changes) is a tonic-dominant pattern.

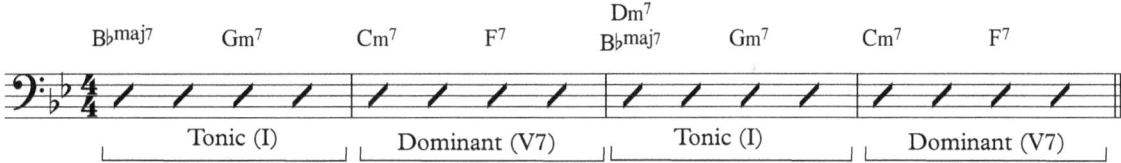

Example 5b

The reduction looks like this:

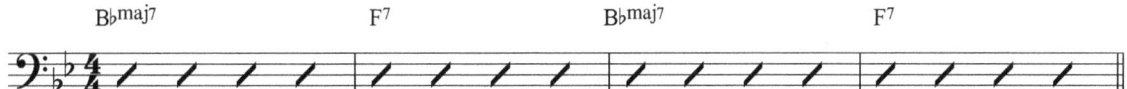

Walking bass application:

It is easiest to create these lines by thinking of the top notes of the tonic and dominant chord. Refer to Chapter 1 on I-V-I harmony, as the same paradigms will be useful here.

175

Example 6a

In this first four bar example a Bb triad, starting from scale degree 1 in the key of the tonic, expresses both the I and vi functions. The V7, starting from scale degree 2 in the key of the tonic, expresses both the ii and V7 functions. This results in a purely diatonic bass line.

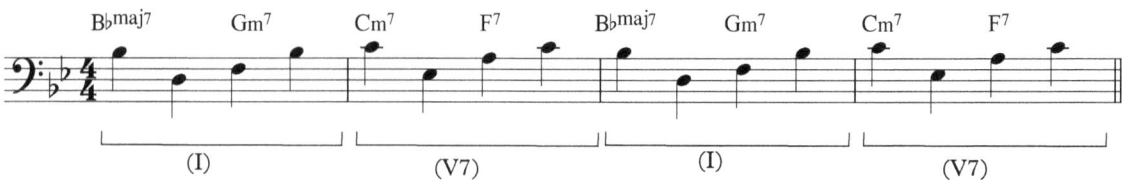

The strong chord tones of Gm7—the 3rd and 7th—are articulated on beats 3 & 4, where the chord changes. It will sound as if the vi chord is deliberately articulated, even without a chordal instrument comping.

Example 6b

Here is the same example, with the melody motion highlighted. It follows a melodic motion of scale degree 1-2-1-2 in the tonic.

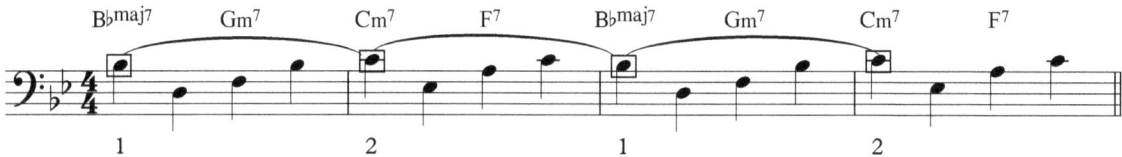

It is possible to apply this concept from scale degrees other than 1 of tonic and 2 of dominant with similar results.

Example 7a

In this example, measure four doesn't articulate the shared notes of ii and V7, but rather outlines the V7 chord exclusively. This effectively ignores the predominant with no negative effect. Instead of two beats each of ii and V7, there are four beats of V7. The strength of the dominant sound will fulfill the harmonic needs of the music, and the ear will both recognize and appreciate the functionality of the line. The melody motion is 3-2-1-7.

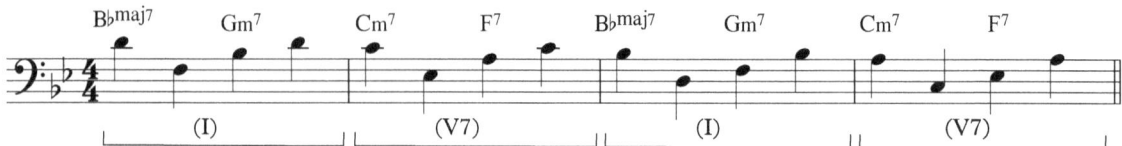

Example 7b

Here's another way to replace ii with V7 entirely. The melody motion is 1-7-1-2. Note the content is still purely diatonic.

Example 7c

This example presents many of the diatonic possibilities one has using I and V7 in their diatonic forms.

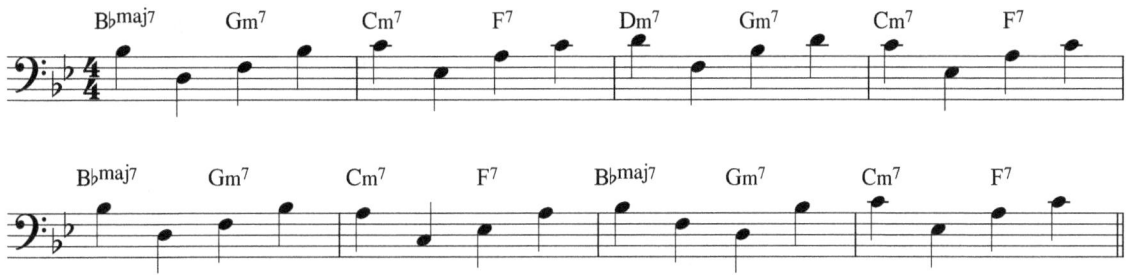

Substitute chord progressions:

There are many different ways to express the A section of rhythm changes. Variations and substitutions allow for the expression of many different types of colors and sounds. Learning the various substitute chord progressions, and recognizing the most appropriate situations to apply the substitutions, can only come through experience.

First and foremost, listen to and transcribe bass lines (by Paul Chambers, Ron Carter, Ray Brown, etc). Play with older and more experienced musicians, and ask them questions; they are a treasured source of information. Consult books like this, The Low Down series, John Goldsby's The Jazz Bass Book, or Killer Walking Bass by Jim Kalbach and Teymur Phell. These are valuable resources for some of the alternate changes you may encounter.

Composing your own bass lines and incorporating your written vocabulary in performance situations is an invaluable learning tool.

Though it is important to know the different rhythm changes variations, being able to recognize and react to these changes is what makes the difference in a performance situation. Sometimes the bassist will infer the substitute changes before they happen; sometimes the soloist will reflect them first. Either way, your ear should govern whether you choose to respond in kind or stick to the "standard" changes.

Example 8

Here is a small sampling of the subtle variations you may encounter over the first 4 bars of rhythm changes.

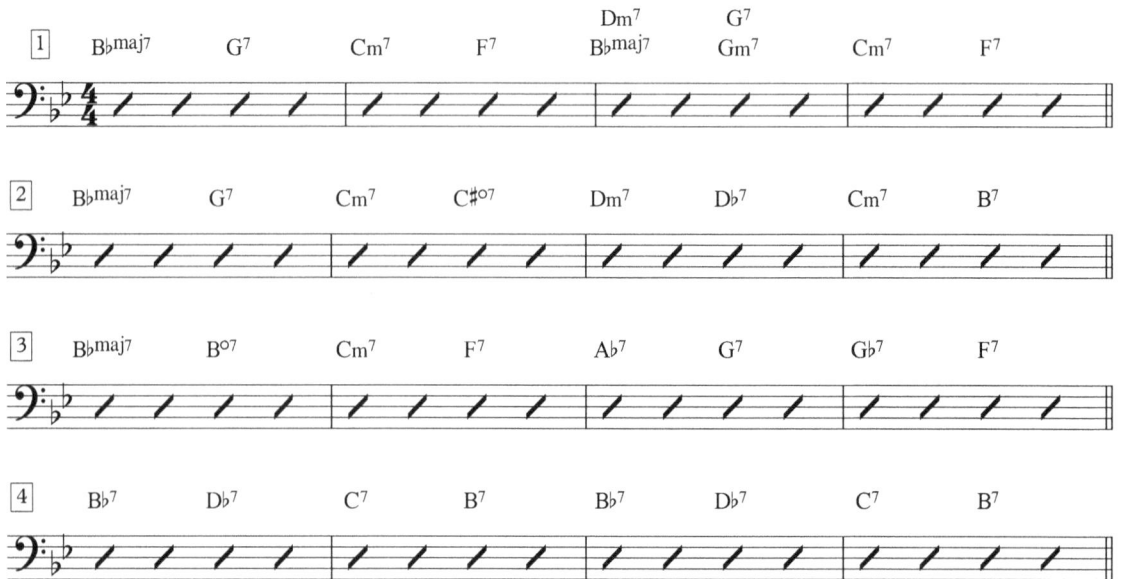

All of these changes are functional and offer a change in color that are appropriate in various musical situations. The first and second variations you see are realistically the most common you'll encounter: changes in the quality of the VI chord.

Reacting to the changes in quality of the VI chord:

If you hear these substitutions, adjusting your bass line to reflect the change in quality can be quite simple. When dealing with chord changes of two beats each, the difference between a Bb Maj7 to a G7 (as opposed to Gm7) is the introduction of a B Natural. This quality change can be accommodated without needing to shift.

Example 9a

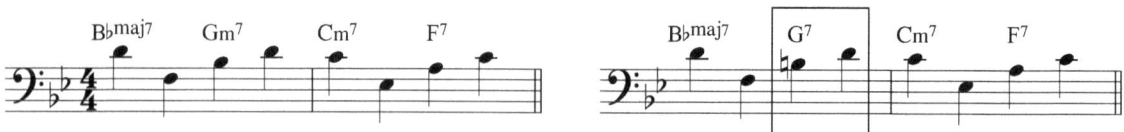

Example 9b

Reduction Harmony results in two shapes: a G7 and F7. The ordering of notes is what still addresses the micro harmony from the previous example.

For these subtle changes in harmony, it may be impossible to react in time to a voicing that's different than what you expected or played. You may articulate the Bb (referencing Gm7) at the same time your pianist comps a G7. These differences are to be expected and is part of the playing experience. If you wait until beat four to articulate the 3rd of the vi or VI chord, you will have enough to react to the established quality.

Example 9c

This example provides a way to delay the introduction of the B natural to beat four. Though this isn't strictly a triadic shape (due to four different notes being used), it shows how you can manipulate the shape to fit the situation with minimal effort.

Using 7b9 over the dominant sounds:

In addition to the changes between the quality of the vi and VI chord, you can also highlight differences between dominant 7 and dominant 7b9. Incorporating the 7b9 shape is a great way to add more color to your bass lines and effectively sequence melodic ideas. The 7b9 chord can be freely exchanged with the V7 chord, and works best when the tension of the b9 falls on beat three.

Example 10a

The 7b9 shape can be applied to the VI chord. Note the shared notes between BbMaj7 (tonic) and G7b9 (dominant VI chord).

BbMaj7 (I)   Bb | D F | A
G7b9 (VI7b9) G B | D F | Ab

Example 10b

The same shape in a different inversion can be used between Dm7 and G7 for the same reasons.

Dm7 (iii) | D F A C |
G7b9 (VI7b9) G B | D F | Ab

Example 11a

Here's a sample bass line to demonstrate sequencing V7b9 through the Section 1 of rhythm changes. The melody motion is 5-4-3-2. Notice the presence of both dominant Shapes A and B.

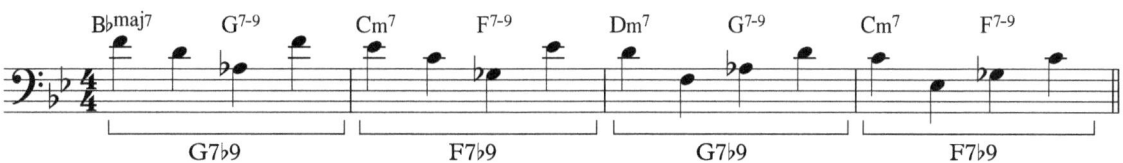

This example is essentially the same as Example 9b, which uses a G7 to F7 shape. The only difference now is the introduction of the b9.

Example 11b

If the second chord were articulated as a Bdim7 instead of a G7—a common substitution—the G7b9 shape would still work, because the core of the G7b9 sound is a B diminished 7 chord.

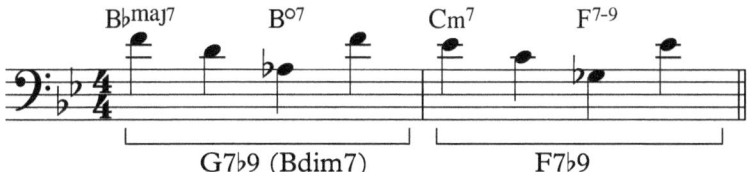

The second A section:

The ending of the second A section is just a slight variation of the first ending. Instead of moving to a ii-V-I back to tonic, the second ending resolves to tonic in the last measure.

Example 12a

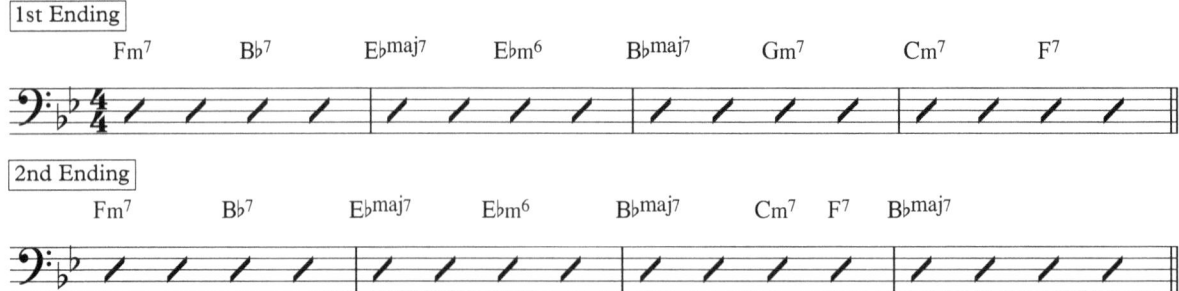

The second ending doesn't provide enough space to apply an entire reduction of the measure, however we can use the I-V-I intervals from Chapter 2 to cover the move from tonic to dominant and back to tonic. That would look like this:

Example 12b

Revisit Chapter 2 to review all two-note options for expressing tonic-dominant-tonic harmonies. There are many melody notes that you can use for this purpose.

Exercises

Exercise 1 - I-VI-ii-V

This exercise demonstrates walking over the many substitute possibilities for I-vi-ii-V.

Section 2: Moving from I to IV:

Section 2 involves the move from I to IV, and eventually back to one. This is the only part of the A section that does not follow the cyclical I-vi-ii-V7 pattern.

Example 13

The move from I to IV does not incorporate new concepts, but rather uses information from the beginning of the chapter. Expressing the move to IV will use the Reduction Harmony technique. We will use the Bb7 shape to articulate the shared notes on beats 1 & 2 of the measure, because Bb7 functions as a dominant of the IV chord. Expressing movement from EbMaj7 to Ebmin6 will reuse the diadic harmony concept from Chapter 2. Use of 6ths fits into the natural aesthetic created by the triadic harmony.

I to IV:

Moving from I to IV, we look for the the positions which articulate the shared notes between Fm7 and Bb7 on beats 1 & 2. These two chords contain two shared notes: F and Ab.

Example 14

These examples use both Shape A and B. See if you can identify which shape is used, and whether the result is diatonic or 7b9.

IV to iv:

Example 15

The move to minor iv was addressed briefly in Chapter 2 on diadic movement. You may even recall the exact chord change happening in the Bb Blues example (Chapter 2, Example 6a):

Measure 6 shows the move from major IV to minor iv using the 6th. Even though many ways exist to express this harmony, we will primarily use 6ths as the basis for application with Reduction Harmony.

Example 16a

This shows a bass line using 6ths then a triadic Eb minor shape to express the shared notes on beats 1 & 2.

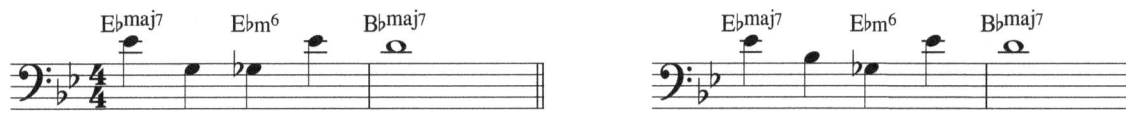

Example 16b

The 6ths can also travel to complete the resolution:

Using Edim7 instead of Ebm6 also incorporates 6ths. As I mentioned in Chapter 3 (Example 22), the symmetry of a diminished chord allows you to think of it as having multiple roots.

Example 17

The first two measures use an Edim7 chord, and the last two use a C#dim7 chord. Notice the voice leading of the melody voice. The first two measures pass chromatically from Eb-E-F. The last two measures uses the Traveling Melody Note concept from Chapter 3, SD 4-#2-3 in the tonic.

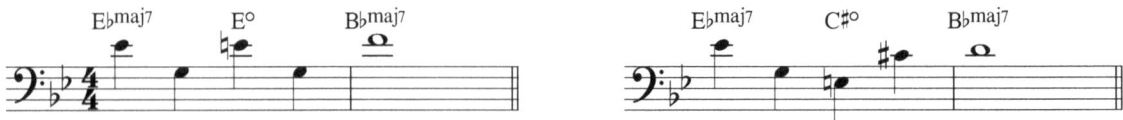

Walking bass application:

Here are just a few applications that incorporate the variations in techniques thus far.

Example 18

Sample Bass Lines

These samples will utilize as many of the Reduction Harmony techniques as possible. Look for the reduction shapes between I and vi, ii and V7, and all of the other possible harmonic substitutions. Experiment with revoicing the arpeggios and reordering notes in these samples—the possibilities are limitless. These samples provide an example of how the Reduction Harmony concept might sound when integrated into a walking bass line with more traditional vocabulary. Traditional vocabulary is incorporated into these samples to provide an example of how the Reduction Harmony concept might sound when integrated into a more traditional walking bass line.

Sample 1 - Rhythm Changes (4 pages)

Sample 1 - Rhythm Changes (4 pages)

Chorus 1

Chorus 2

Chorus 3

Chorus 4

www.ingramcontent.com/pod-product-compliance
Lightning Source LLC
Chambersburg PA
CBHW062129160426
43191CB00013B/2246